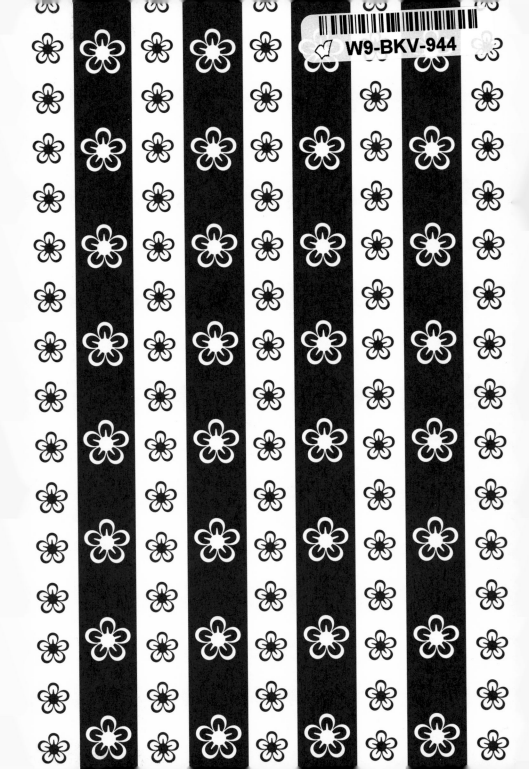

Donna Smalley

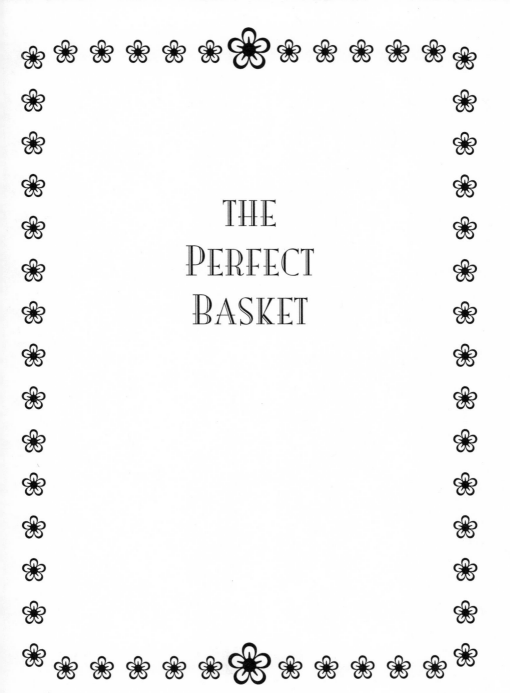

THE
PERFECT
BASKET

THE

PERFECT

BASKET

Make

Your Own

Special Occasion

Baskets

DIANE PHILLIPS

Hearst Books
New York

TO CHUCK,

FOR TWENTY-THREE YEARS OF CONSTANT FUN,

AND TO CARRIE AND RYAN

FOR COMING ALONG FOR THE RIDE.

It is the policy of William Morrow and Company, Inc., and its imprints and
affiliates, recognizing the importance of preserving what has been written, to
print the books we publish on acid-free paper, and we exert our
best efforts to that end.

LIBRARY OF CONGRESS CATALOGING-IN-PUBLICATION DATA

Phillips, Diane
The perfect basket: make your own special occasion baskets/
Diane Phillips
p. cm
Includes index.
ISBN: 0-688-13031-3
1. Handicraft. 2. Gifts. 3. Baskets. 4. Cookery. I. Title.
TT157.P465 1994
745.5—dc20   94-6974
CIP

Printed in United States of America
FIRST EDITION

1   3   5   7   9   10   8   6   4   2

BOOK DESIGN BY FLY PRODUCTIONS

Acknowledgments

This book could not have been written without the help and encouragement of some very special people. To my friend and agent Susan Travis, who continues to help make my dreams a reality, a special thank you. Thanks also to all the elves at the McBride Agency: David, Winifred, and Margret for their assistance and expertise.

Throughout the writing and shaping of this book, Harriet Bell has been more than an editor — she has been mentor, mother, and friend. She has given me her wisdom and friendship, and listened to my whining. To Robbie Capp, copy editor extraordinaire, I want to express my appreciation for your enormous skill in putting the manuscript into its final form. A special thank you to Susan Goldman for the beautiful jacket photograph.

Some special friends have given me their love and caring during this process, and I want to thank Craig and Andrea White, Nancy and Mike Stansbury, Chris and Ann Priebe, Linda and Dennis Costello, Carolyn and David Clark for being encouragers and for tasting everything! A large thank you to Jana Cason and the staff at J.C.'s Kitchen Company here in San Diego for allowing me to come into their kitchen and do what I love.

Contents

Introduction

Buying prepackaged gift baskets is convenient but expensive. The convenience is in having the items all wrapped and arranged in a basket filled with straw and sealed with cellophane and pretty ribbons. Unfortunately, when the wrapping and straw are removed, the recipient often discovers that the items aren't very useful or of very high quality.

For a little more time and a lot less money, I'll show how to assemble your own one-of-a kind gift baskets. Commercially produced baskets just don't compare with the personally selected basket that you can create for a fraction of the cost, with quality ingredients tailored to a friend's tastes and interests. *The Perfect Basket* shows how to put together unique budget-minded baskets. I've also included deluxe baskets for special occasions — bon voyage, honeymoon, get well — in these pages. But there, too, by assembling your own, the cost will be considerably less than purchasing a similar store-bought ensemble.

Since my background is in cooking, I offer food-centered gifts in the first section. Most of these baskets feature a homemade mix and accompanying recipe combined with accessories for use in preparing or serving the suggested food dish. Others include recipes that you prepare for the basket.

Special occasion baskets that hold gifts other than food are found in the second section, each related to a particular theme. Included are those small gifts we often need as a thank you or to mark a special event in someone's life. Instead of giving a single article, if you pack an unusual container with a few useful items, the recipient will be reminded of your thoughtfulness many times over.

I use the term *basket* in this book to include containers other than traditional baskets. I encourage you to take the same creative approach when searching for unusual receptacles for your gifts. When you look around for novel containers think about recycling. Chances are you have some ideal resources in your garage or attic. Tag sales and flea markets are great sources, too.

Be guided by your friends' personal likes and lifestyles, and you can come up with original gifts to delight everyone on your list.

Supplies

Finding baskets and the items to fill them is as easy as going to department stores, grocers, import stores, and shopping through catalogs. Variety is the key here. Mixing and matching colors and themes is what makes these gifts so much fun to put together.

Packaging materials are readily available in greeting card stores, as well as floral and craft stores. Colored tissue is most versatile as stuffing for outer wraps and layered for decorative effects. Also look for clear and colored cellophane bags (used by florists for packing corsages) in floral and craft stores. For baked goods, boxes,

decorated tins, and wax-lined bags with color-coordinated ribbons and wraps can be found in greeting card stores. Cake-decorating stores are also a source for baked-goods boxes.

Glass jars and containers are stocked by many department stores as well as import stores, but recycling jars is a more creative and economical way to give gifts. Mustard and jam jars make nice containers for spice blends. Imported beer bottles and green Perrier or dark blue mineral water bottles are ideal for homemade vinegar blends. Wash the jars or bottles in warm soapy water and soak off the labels. Stubborn glue marks can be removed with liquid solvent called DeSolvit. For a festive, inexpensive gift, cover jar tops in seasonal fabric cut with pinking shears and tie with color-matched ribbon.

A Source Guide at the back of this book lists outlets that are favorites of mine for functional and unusual baskets and other containers. Also listed are sources for some cooking supplies that may not be readily available where you live. For example, some relatively new items included in the baking mixes are cultured buttermilk powder and pure vanilla powder. These dried powders are added to the food mixes, just like flour, sugar, or spices. Both of these products are of the highest quality and may be found in your local grocery stores, but if not, addresses and phone numbers for mail-order purchase are in the Source Guide.

 # FOOD

B A S K E T S

I began giving food gifts many years ago by filling unusual containers with my own homemade mixes. Then I started adding an implement or two when a particular mix called for tools that a friend might not have had. For a more elaborate gift, I included serving or table accessories geared to the food dishes to be prepared from my mixes. As you'll see, the food baskets in this book differ from those found in gourmet shops by the degree of personalization you can bring to each one.

The variety of containers you have to choose from in preparing food baskets is endless. Soup tureens, salad spinners, salad bowls, stockpots, cookie jars, teapots, ice buckets, water pitchers, colanders, canisters — and baskets of infinite variety — all make useful containers for culinary gifts. (You'll find still more container ideas in the second part of this book.)

The format of the food baskets section includes recipes that can be made from the homemade mix that you'll prepare for your gift package. These recipes should be given with your mix on a recipe card or gift tag attached to it. If you have a computer, design your own recipe cards and print out copies as you need them. If hand lettering is your specialty, put your talent to good use. For smaller recipe tags, a photocopy shop can reduce your design so that four copies will fit onto a standard 8 1/2- by 11-inch sheet of paper. Your master sheet then contains four copies of the recipe. Select a color of card stock that coordinates with the basket and attach the reduced-size recipe to it.

Happy gifting!

Cookie Monster's Basket

C hildren love a chance to experiment in the kitchen, and what better way to inspire creativity than to give a basket filled with goodies for cookie baking. Select a large, colorful plastic basket that can be recycled for art supplies or toys. Include the Gingerperson Cookie Mix and Candy Cookie Mix along with cookie cutters, decorative sprinkles, cake decorating tubes in assorted colors, chocolate chips, a small rolling pin, child-size chef apron, and pot holder. And don't forget a paper toque-blanche (chef's hat), available at professional restaurant stores. This basket can be tailored to the season by lining it with calendar-coordinated fabric and including appropriate cookie cutters. For example: orange-black for an October gift, with pumpkin and witch cookie cutters; a pretty pastel gingham with floral cookie cutters for a June gift. Bags of cookie mix given with cookie cutters make unique birthday party favors.

Gingerperson Cookie Mix

Makes 2 1/2 cups

This little guy/gal brings good taste and good cheer because there's a smile on his/her face. The dough is easy to work with and the cookies have a mild ginger flavor.

1/2 cup dark brown sugar	3/4 teaspoon ground cinnamon
2 cups all-purpose flour	1/2 teaspoon baking soda
1 1/4 teaspoons ground ginger	

Combine the ingredients in a medium bowl and blend until they are evenly distributed. Store in an airtight container.

Gingerperson
Cookies

Makes 2 dozen 3-inch cookies

1/2 cup (1 stick) unsalted butter or margarine, softened

1/4 cup dark molasses

1/2 package (2 1/2 cups) Gingerperson Cookie Mix (PAGE 3)

Preheat the oven to 350° F. In the large bowl of an electric mixer, cream the butter and add the molasses. Beat in the cookie mix and mix until blended. Halve the dough and flatten into one-inch-thick rounds. Wrap in plastic wrap and chill for 2 hours. Roll the dough onto a lightly floured board to 1/4 inch thickness, and cut with a floured 3-inch cookie cutter. Place one inch apart on ungreased cookie sheets. Bake for 12 minutes or until the edges are lightly browned. Cool for two minutes, then transfer to wire racks to cool.

Candy Cookie
Mix

Makes approximately 3 cups

A versatile cookie mix that lends itself to imaginative creations, such as the Reese's peanut butter cups variation or Butterfinger version. Include a small bag of the appropriate candy in the basket.

1/2 cup sugar	1 teaspoon baking soda
1/2 cup brown sugar	2 cups all-purpose flour
1 teaspoon powdered vanilla	

Combine all the ingredients in a medium bowl. Whisk the ingredients together until they are evenly distributed, making sure all brown sugar lumps are crushed. Store the mixture in an airtight container.

Candy Cookies

Makes 3 dozen cookies

1 cup (2 sticks) unsalted butter or margarine, softened	1 cup candy bar chunks (Reese's peanut butter cups cut into quarters, Butterfinger
1 large egg	bars cut into chunks, white-chocolate
1 package Candy Cookie Mix (PAGE 4)	chunks, or milk-chocolate chunks)

Preheat the oven to 350° F. In the large bowl of an electric mixer, beat the butter until it is smooth. Add the egg, and continue beating until the egg is combined. Add the Candy Cookie Mix and candy bar chunks, and blend on low just until the cookie mix is incorporated. Form the cookies into 1 1/2-inch balls and place them 2 inches apart on an ungreased cookie sheet. Bake for 10 to 12 minutes, until golden on the edges. Remove from the oven, allow to rest for 2 minutes, and then transfer to a wire rack to cool.

Cookie Connoisseur's Basket

Most grown-ups love sweets as much as kids do. A basket of assorted homemade cookies is an especially nice way to thank a dinner host or to welcome new neighbors. Instead of putting cookies in a basket, how about a cookie jar? Or look for tag sale finds: an earthenware bean crock, a wide-necked Victorian teapot, a metal milk pail, or a fish bowl. The cookies that follow are definite crowd pleasers, so be sure to include all three recipes — White Chocolate Macadamia Nut Wonders, Amaretto Shortbread, and White Chocolate Chunk Cookies — with your gift.

Mrs. Phillips' White Chocolate Macadamia Nut Wonders

Makes 4 dozen cookies

These cookies will remind you of the ones sold at upscale bakeries — except for the price, which will be much lower from your own oven.

1 cup (2 sticks) unsalted butter, softened	2 1/4 cups all-purpose flour
1 cup brown sugar	1 teaspoon baking soda
3/4 cup white sugar	12 ounces white-chocolate chips
2 large eggs	(or coarsely chopped white chocolate)
2 teaspoons vanilla extract	2 cups chopped macadamia nuts
	1 1/2 cups flaked coconut

Preheat the oven to 350° F. In the large bowl of an electric mixer, cream the butter and sugars. Add the eggs and vanilla and blend until smooth. Add the flour, baking soda, chips, nuts, and coconut, and mix until just blended. Roll the dough into golf-ball size and place about 1 1/2 inches apart on foil- or waxed-paper-lined cookie sheets. Bake for 9 to 12 minutes, or until light golden brown. Transfer to a wire rack and cool.

Amaretto

Shortbread

Makes 5 dozen cookies

This distinctive shortbread, a winner at our house, adds a nice touch to a basket of assorted cookies or can be given with a shortbread mold and a bottle of amaretto, almond-flavored liqueur.

1 cup (2 sticks) unsalted butter, softened	1/4 cup amaretto liqueur
1 cup sugar, plus 2 tablespoons	2 cups all-purpose flour
1 large egg, separated	2/3 cup sliced almonds

Preheat the oven to 325°F. and line a 15 1/2- by 10 1/2- by 1-inch jelly-roll pan with foil. In a medium mixing bowl, cut the butter into 1 cup sugar. Add the egg yolk and 3 tablespoons of the amaretto. Stir in the flour and pat the dough into the jelly-roll pan. Beat the egg white with the remaining tablespoon of amaretto and brush the dough evenly with the mixture. Distribute the almonds over the top of the shortbread and sprinkle the remaining sugar over the almonds. Bake for 40 minutes, or until the shortbread is golden in color. Cut into squares while still warm.

White Chocolate Chunk Cookies

Makes 4 dozen cookies

These rich cookies are soft and chewy with the dual bold taste of cocoa and smooth taste of white chocolate. A rich addition to an assortment of baked goods or given by themselves, these cookies are popular with all ages.

1/2 cups (3 sticks) unsalted butter, softened
1/2 cup brown sugar
1/2 cup white sugar
3 teaspoons vanilla extract
2 large eggs

12 teaspoons baking soda
1 cup cocoa
3 1/2 cups all-purpose flour
12 ounces white-chocolate chips (or coarsely chopped white-chocolate chunks)

Preheat the oven to 350° F. In the large bowl of an electric mixer, cream the butter and sugars until fluffy. Mix in the vanilla and eggs. Slowly mix in the baking soda, cocoa, flour, and chips. Drop full tablespoons of the mixture onto foil-lined baking sheets about 2 inches apart. Bake for 10 to 12 minutes. Remove from the oven and let sit on cookie sheets for 2 minutes. Remove cookies to racks to cool.

A Loaf of Bread Basket

Three deliciously different bread mixes make this a baker's bounty as a wedding shower or housewarming gift. Give these bread mixes in a large earthenware bowl that can be used for mixing the dough and include a serrated knife and cutting board. Or line a long bread basket with a crisp white linen napkin and nestle in it your three homemade bread mixes, plus a set of collectible butter knives or molds.

Old-fashioned Herbed Oatmeal Bread Mix

Makes 5 1/2 cups

This bread is delicious for sandwiches or toast. It has a pronounced herb flavor that enhances chicken or fresh vegetable sandwiches.

1 envelope active dry yeast	1/2 teaspoon dried thyme
1/2 cup old-fashioned rolled oats	1/2 teaspoon dried sage
3 tablespoons buttermilk powder	1 cup whole wheat flour
1 tablespoon sugar	4 cups all-purpose flour
1 teaspoon dried dillweed	1 teaspoon salt

In a large mixing bowl, whisk together all the ingredients until they are evenly distributed. Store the mixture in an airtight container.

Old-fashioned Herbed
Oatmeal Bread

Makes 2 loaves

1 package Old-fashioned Herbed	1 large egg
Oatmeal Bread Mix (PAGE 9)	2 tablespoons butter or margarine,
3/4 cup lukewarm water (105° — 115°)	melted
1 1/4 cups milk	Additional flour for kneading

Preheat the oven to 375° F. Place the bread mix in the large bowl of an electric mixer. Add the water and milk and begin to mix with a dough hook. Add the egg, and continue to beat the mixture until it comes away from the bowl and forms a ball. If the dough is too sticky, add 2 tablespoons of flour and continue to beat the dough, adding additional flour if needed. If the dough is too dry, add 1 tablespoon of water, and then additional water if needed. Turn the dough out onto a floured board, and knead for 5 minutes, until it is shiny and elastic. Place the dough into a greased bowl, turning to coat each side. Let the dough rise for 1 hour, or until it is doubled in size. Punch the dough down, divide it into two, and form it into two loaves. Place in greased loaf pans, or if you prefer, shape the bread into rounds and place on greased cookie sheets. Cover the dough and let it rise another 45 minutes to one hour, until it has doubled in bulk. Brush with butter, and bake the bread in a preheated oven for 30 to 40 minutes, or until it sounds hollow when tapped. Remove the pans to wire racks to cool. Remove the loaves from the pans.

Banana Chocolate-Chip Streusel Bread

A take-off on traditional banana bread, this quick bread combines chocolate chips and bran cereal with a crunchy streusel topping for a delicious snack bread.

Streusel Topping Mix

Makes 3/4 cup

1/3 cup all-purpose flour   1/2 teaspoon ground cinnamon
1/2 cup sugar

Combine and blend the ingredients in a small bowl. Store in an airtight container.

Banana Chocolate-Chip Bread Mix

Makes 3 1/4 cups

1 cup bran cereal   1/2 cup chocolate chips
1 1/3 cups all-purpose flour   1 tablespoon baking powder
1/3 cup sugar   1 teaspoon vanilla powder

Combine and blend the ingredients in a medium bowl. Store in an airtight container.

Streusel Topping

Frosts 1 loaf

1/4 cup (1/2 stick) unsalted butter or margarine cut into 1/2-inch chunks

1 package Streusel Topping Mix (PAGE *11*)

In a small mixing bowl, cut the butter into the streusel topping mix until the mixture resembles small peas. Set aside while making the bread batter.

Banana Chocolate-Chip Streusel Bread

Makes 1 loaf

1 package Banana Chocolate-Chip Bread Mix (PAGE *11*)
1/2 cup milk
2 ripe bananas, mashed

1 large egg
1/4 cup canola oil
1 recipe Streusel Topping

Preheat the oven to 400° F. and grease a standard-size loaf pan. Place the bread mix in a large mixing bowl. Gradually add the milk, bananas, egg, and oil, stirring with a wooden spoon until the batter is smooth. Pour the batter into the prepared loaf pan and top with the Streusel Topping. Bake for 20 to 25 minutes, or until a toothpick inserted into the center of the bread comes out clean. Remove the bread from the oven to a wire rack and allow it to cool. Remove from the loaf pan and serve at room temperature, or refrigerate and serve cold.

Cornmeal and Molasses Bread Mix

Makes 4 cups

As a child, I loved to eat this bread toasted, spread with copious amounts of apple butter. Whether you eat it for breakfast or slice it for sandwiches, you will love its unique flavor.

1/2 cup yellow cornmeal   3 1/2 cups all-purpose flour
2 teaspoons salt   1/2 cup whole wheat flour
1 package active dry yeast

Combine all the ingredients in a medium bowl and blend until they are evenly distributed. Store in an airtight container.

Cornmeal and Molasses Bread

Makes 1 loaf

1 package Cornmeal and Molasses   1/4 cup molasses
Bread Mix   2 tablespoons unsalted butter or
1 1/4 cups warm milk (105° —115°)   margarine, melted

Preheat the oven to 375° F. and grease a 9- by 5-inch loaf pan. Place the bread mix in a large mixing bowl. Make a well in the mix and add the milk, molasses, and butter. Stir with a wooden spoon until the dough forms a ball. Turn out onto a floured board and knead for 8 minutes. Place the dough in a greased bowl, and cover it. Let the dough rise until it has doubled in bulk. Punch the dough down and shape it into a loaf. Place it into the greased pan. Allow to rise for about 45 minutes, or until doubled in size. Bake the bread for about 40 minutes. Remove the bread from the oven and cool on a wire rack.

Weekend Breakfast Basket

I f you're invited to be a houseguest for a country weekend, here's an appropriately abundant gift for your hosts: all the makings for a delicious breakfast. Start by including homemade Maple Granola and Cranberry Oat Scone Mix. Provide fresh oranges for juice, a bag of coffee beans, a coffee grinder, an assortment of herb teas, and Devonshire cream for the scones. Pack them all in a beribboned wicker hamper.

Maple Granola

Makes 8 1/4 cups

1/4 cup slivered almonds	2/3 cup golden raisins
1 1/3 cups flaked coconut	2/3 cup chopped dates
3 1/2 cups old-fashioned rolled oats	1/2 cup chopped dried apples
1/3 cup vegetable oil	1/3 cup chopped dried apricots
1 cup maple syrup	

Preheat the oven to 350° F. Toast the almonds and coconut in a jelly-roll pan for 10 minutes, or until the coconut is brown. Transfer to a bowl to cool. Toast the oats, stirring occasionally, for 20 minutes and add to the bowl. In a small saucepan, heat the oil and maple syrup until hot, and pour over the oat mixture. Toss the mixture well and bake for 15 minutes. Let the mixture cool and transfer to a bowl. Add the remaining ingredients. Store the granola in an airtight container.

Cranberry Oat Scone Mix

Makes 3 cups

1 cup old-fashioned rolled oats	1 teaspoon baking powder
3/4 cup all-purpose flour	1 cup dried cranberries
1/4 cup sugar	

Combine and blend the ingredients in a small bowl. Store in an airtight container.

Cranberry Oat Scones

Makes 10 to 12

1 package Cranberry Oat Scone Mix (PAGE *14*)

6 tablespoons unsalted butter, cut into pieces

1/4 cup heavy cream

2 tablespoons milk

2 tablespoons sugar

Preheat the oven to 350° F. Place the Cranberry Oat Scone Mix in a small mixing bowl. Cut in the butter until the mixture resembles coarse meal. Sprinkle the heavy cream over the mixture and blend until a ball of dough begins to form. (Add more cream, one teaspoon at a time, if the dough is dry.) Turn the dough onto a floured board and roll about 1/2 inch thick. Cut out 10 rounds with a 2-inch biscuit cutter and reroll any scraps, then cut out additional scones. Place on a lightly greased baking sheet and brush the tops with milk, then sprinkle with sugar. Bake for 15 to 20 minutes, until golden brown. Cool on a wire rack.

Pizza Pizzaz Basket

A welcome tool in any kitchen is the long-handled wooden board called a pizza peel; it's a great base on which to assemble a package of homemade Pizza Dough Mix, a stoneware crock filled with Italian Herb Mix (PAGE *21*) a package of dried tomatoes, and a pizza cutter, held together under clear cellophane. Decorate the top with red and green ribbons for an Italian accent.

Pizza Dough Mix

Makes 6 1/4 cups

2 packages active dry yeast

2 teaspoons sugar

6 cups all-purpose flour

1 1/2 teaspoons salt

Combine the ingredients in a medium bowl, and blend until they are evenly distributed. Store in an airtight container.

Pizza

Makes 2 14-inch pizzas

2 cups warm water (105° – 115°)

2 tablespoons olive oil

1/2 cup freshly grated Parmesan cheese

1 package Pizza Dough Mix

1 1/2 cups pizza sauce

1 cup grated mozzarella

In a bowl, combine the water, oil, Parmesan cheese, and Pizza Dough Mix. Beat with a wooden spoon until the mixture forms a ball. Turn out onto a floured board. Knead until smooth and elastic. Place the dough in a greased bowl. Let rise until doubled in bulk. Preheat the oven to 425° F. Divide the dough in half. Roll it into two 14-inch circles. Lightly oil pizza pans. Lay the dough into the pans. Top with sauce and mozzarella cheese. Bake for 15 to 20 minutes, or until the cheese is golden and the crust is crisp.

Bed-and-Breakfast Tray

Here's a most charming wedding or anniversary present: a breakfast tray, a pair of champagne flutes, a bottle of sparkling cider, two kinds of homemade popover mixes, a little vase with flowers, and a book of Shakespeare's sonnets.

Cherry Pecan Popover Mix

Makes 2 cups

1 cup all-purpose flour	2 tablespoons sugar
1 teaspoon ground cinnamon	1/2 cup dried cherries
1/2 teaspoon ground ginger	1/3 cup chopped pecans

Combine and blend the ingredients in a small bowl. Store in an airtight container.

Cherry Pecan Popovers

Makes 6 popovers

1 package Cherry Pecan Popover Mix	2 tablespoons unsalted butter or
1 cup milk	margarine, melted
2 large eggs	

Preheat the oven to 450° F. Grease 6 popover cups or individual custard cups and place them in the oven to preheat. In a bowl, blend the Cherry Pecan Popover Mix with the milk, eggs, and butter. Pour the batter into the preheated cups and bake for 15 minutes. Reduce the heat to 350° F. and continue to bake for 15 to 20 minutes, or until puffed and browned. Serve warm with butter and jam.

Date and Walnut Popover Mix

Makes 1 1/2 cups

1 cup all-purpose flour 1/3 cup chopped dates

2 tablespoons sugar 1/4 cup chopped walnuts

Combine and blend the ingredients in a small bowl. Store in an airtight container.

Date and Walnut Popovers

Makes 6 popovers

1 package Date and Walnut Popover Mix 2 tablespoons unsalted butter , melted

1 cup milk Ripe Brie cheese, at room temperature

2 large eggs

Preheat the oven to 450° F. Grease 6 popover cups or Pyrex custard cups and place them in the oven to preheat. In a mixing bowl, blend the Date and Walnut Popover Mix with the milk, eggs, and butter. Pour the batter into the preheated cups, and bake for 15 minutes. Reduce the heat to 350° F. and continue to bake for 15 to 20 minutes, or until puffed and browned. Remove from the oven and serve with Brie.

Lettuce Entertain You

A college grad setting up his or her first apartment will welcome this basic entertaining equipment. Start with a large Lucite or wooden salad bowl, line it with a muslin lettuce bag, then fill it with a coordinating Lucite (or wooden) pepper mill, salad tongs, a bottle each of balsamic vinegar and extra-virgin olive oil, and packages of the delicious salad herb blends that follow. Wrap up the filled bowl in a big chef's apron, using the bib and waist apron strings to tie it neatly together.

Tarragon Dressing Mix

Makes scant 1 cup

Herb blends keep well in glass jars with airtight seals or in cruets with stoppers.

1/2 cup dried tarragon	2 teaspoons salt
1/4 cup dried thyme leaves	1 teaspoon freshly ground pepper
2 tablespoons dry mustard	

Combine and blend the ingredients in a small bowl. Store in an airtight container.

Tarragon Dressing

Makes 1 1/4 cups

2 tablespoons fresh lemon juice	1 tablespoon Tarragon Dressing Mix
1/2 teaspoon balsamic vinegar	1 cup olive oil

In a mixing bowl, whisk together the lemon juice and vinegar. Blend in the Tarragon Dressing Mix, and gradually add the oil, whisking until the mixture is smooth and creamy.

Dilled Dressing Mix

Makes 2 cups

This dressing is tasty when served on mixed greens, or tossed into a pasta salad with seafood or chicken. It also makes a dip for fresh raw vegetables.

1/2 cup dried dillweed	1/4 cup dried tarragon
1/2 cup dried minced onion	2 tablespoons garlic powder
1/3 cup dried parsley	1 tablespoon freshly ground black pepper
1/4 cup dried basil	1 teaspoon dried lemon peel

Combine the ingredients in a small bowl and blend until they are evenly distributed. Store in an airtight container.

Dilled Dressing

Makes 1 1/4 cups

3/4 cup mayonnaise	1 1/2 teaspoons Dilled Dressing Mix
1/2 cup milk	

In a small mixing bowl, whisk together the mayonnaise and milk. Add the Dilled Dressing Mix, and whisk until the mixture is smooth. Refrigerate for 2 hours before serving.

Dilled Dip

Makes 1 1/2 cups

1 cup sour cream or low-fat yogurt	1 1/2 tablespoons Dilled Dressing Mix
1/2 cup mayonnaise or low-fat mayonnaise	

In a small glass mixing bowl, whisk together the sour cream and mayonnaise. Fold in the Dilled Dressing Mix and whisk until the mixture is combined. Refrigerate for 2 hours before serving.

Italian Herb Mix

Makes 1/2 cup

This versatile blend can be used to make a creamy Italian or oil-and-vinegar-based dressing. Sprinkle the herbs over pizzas, into pasta sauces, or blend with butter for an Italian herb butter to spread on bread or grilled fish.

1/4 cup dried basil

2 tablespoons dried oregano

1 teaspoon dried fennel seed, crushed

1 tablespoon dried parsley

2 teaspoons garlic powder

1/2 teaspoon freshly ground black pepper

1 teaspoon sugar

Combine the ingredients in a small bowl and blend until they are evenly distributed. Store in an airtight container.

Creamy Italian Dressing

Makes 1 1/4 cups

1 cup mayonnaise

2 tablespoons chopped onion

2 tablespoons red wine vinegar

1 tablespoon Italian Herb Mix

In a small mixing bowl, combine the mayonnaise with the remaining ingredients, and whisk until the dressing is smooth. Refrigerate for at least one hour before serving. Serve over greens or as a dip for raw vegetables.

Italian Herb Dressing

Makes 1 1/3 cups

1 cup olive oil

1/3 cup balsamic vinegar

1 tablespoon Italian Herb Mix

In a small glass bowl, whisk together the oil, vinegar, and Italian Herb Mix until blended. Refrigerate before serving.

Flavored Vinegar Basket

L ong before recycling became fashionable in America, the thrifty French routinely reused wine bottles for storing homemade vinegar. Expensive to buy, inexpensive to make, fine vinegars are basic to a gourmet kitchen. Blend a version offered here and present it in a recycled wine bottle, together with a container of olive oil encased in a salad spinner.

Mixed Bouquet Vinegar

Makes 1 quart

1 cup fresh herbs, such as rosemary, chervil, thyme, basil, or oregano
4 to 5 whole black peppercorns

1 large clove garlic, peeled and split
1 quart white wine vinegar

Place the herbs in a clean one-quart glass bottle. Add the peppercorns and garlic. Pour the vinegar almost to the top to fill. Cap and seal. Let stand in a warm, sunny area for up to 2 weeks to infuse. Give this in a good-looking bottle and attach a recipe card for your favorite vinaigrette.

House Vinaigrette

Makes 3/4 cup

1/4 cup herb vinegar
1/2 teaspoon Dijon mustard
1/2 cup olive oil

1/2 teaspoon salt
1 clove garlic, mashed

In a large bowl, whisk the vinegar and mustard. Gradually add the oil until the mixture is smooth. Add the salt and garlic and blend well. Refrigerate for at least 3 hours before using.

Cinnamon Spice Vinegar

Makes 2 cups

Use this vinegar in poultry marinades and as a complement to composed fruit salads.

2 cups white vinegar
2 whole cinnamon sticks
6 cloves garlic
1 tablespoon dried orange peel

Combine all the ingredients in a clean glass jar with an airtight seal. Let sit in a cool, dry place for 7 days. Strain into a clear jar with a tight-fitting lid.

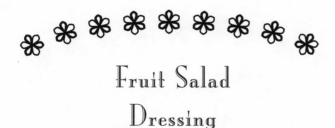

Fruit Salad Dressing

Makes 1 1/2 cups

1 cup vegetable oil
1/3 cup Cinnamon Spice Vinegar
2 tablespoons chopped parsley
2 tablespoons honey
2 heads radicchio, cleaned and separated
1 avocado, peeled and cut into 8 wedges
2 large navel oranges, cut into sections

Whisk together the oil and Cinnamon Spice Vinegar in a glass bowl. Add the parsley and honey. Arrange the radicchio with the avocado wedges and orange sections, placing the fruit in a fan shape over the radicchio. Drizzle each salad with three tablespoons of dressing.

Fruit-Flavored Vinegar

Makes 1 quart

Fruit-flavored vinegar, usually served only in four-star restaurants, makes an unusual and colorful gift. Berries, apples, peaches, nectarines, and plums can all be used for the flavoring. (Do not mix fruits.) I recommend using frozen fruit (unsweetened) if fresh fruit, especially out of season, is too costly.

1 quart white vinegar

2 cups fruit

In a glass bowl, pour the white vinegar over the fruit. Let the mixture stand at room temperature overnight. Drain the vinegar and decant in a clean glass container.

Fruity
Vinaigrette

Makes 1 3/4 cups

1/4 cup Fruit-Flavored Vinegar	1 teaspoon Dijon mustard
1/2 cup sugar	2 tablespoons poppy seeds
1/2 teaspoon salt	2/3 cup canola oil
1/4 cup chopped onion	

In a small bowl, whisk together the ingredients, until they are blended. Refrigerate the dressing until ready to use. Serve over Bibb lettuce with mandarin oranges, sliced red onions, and slivered almonds.

Soup's On! Basket

The warmest of gifts — literally and figuratively — is wonderful homemade soup. The mixes that you prepare can be transformed quickly by their recipient into a hearty meal — an especially helpful gift for an under-the-weather or otherwise housebound friend. This basket is actually a soup tureen filled with soup mixes, and you might also add a bread mix (PAGES *9-13*). Top it off with a useful soup ladle.

Spicy Lentil Soup Mix

Makes 2 1/4 cups

This spicy soup will warm up a cold winter's night. It freezes well — but it's doubtful that you'll have any leftovers.

2 cups lentils	4 chicken bouillon cubes, crumbled
1/8 teaspoon cayenne pepper	1 bay leaf
1/2 teaspoon cumin seed	1 teaspoon garlic powder

Combine the ingredients in a small bowl and blend until they are evenly distributed. Store in an airtight container.

Spicy Lentil Soup

Serves 6

2 tablespoons vegetable oil
1 cup chopped onion
2 cloves garlic, crushed
2 carrots, chopped

2 celery ribs, sliced
2 quarts water
1 package Spicy Lentil Soup Mix (PAGE *25*)
1/2 pound kielbasa, or Polish sausage

Put the oil in a stockpot, then sauté the onion, garlic, carrots, and celery until they become soft. Add the water, Spicy Lentil Soup Mix, and kielbasa. Bring the soup to a boil, reduce the heat, cover, and simmer for 2 hours. Remove the bay leaf before serving. Serve with crusty bread.

Yellow Split Pea Soup Mix

Makes 2 cups

This soup mix makes a great presentation when it is layered in a glass jar.

2 cups yellow split peas
1 bay leaf
2 chicken bouillon cubes, crumbled

2 teaspoons dried marjoram
1 teaspoon salt
1/4 teaspoon white pepper

Layer the ingredients in an airtight container.

Yellow Split Pea Soup

Serves 6

2 tablespoons butter
1 medium onion, sliced
1 1/2 cups sliced carrots
3/4 cup chopped celery

2 1/2 quarts water
1 package Yellow Split Pea
Soup Mix (PAGE *26*)

Melt the butter in a heavy soup kettle over medium low heat, and cook the onion, carrots, and celery until they begin to soften. Add the water and the Yellow Split Pea Soup Mix and bring to a boil. Then reduce the heat to a simmer, and cover for about 3 hours. Season the soup with additional salt if needed.

Wild Rice Soup Mix

Makes 1 1/4 cups

Did you know that wild rice is not rice, but an aquatic grass harvested in Minnesota and Canada? It makes an elegant soup that is also hearty and satisfying. Pack the wild rice in a separate container from the spice mix.

1 cup wild rice

Pack the wild rice in an airtight container.

Spice
Mixture

5 chicken bouillon cubes, crumbled	1 teaspoon dried thyme
1 teaspoon curry powder	1/2 teaspoon white pepper
1/2 teaspoon dry mustard	1/4 cup all-purpose flour

Combine and blend the ingredients in a small bowl. Store in an airtight container.

Wild Rice
Soup

Serves 6 to 8

1 package Wild Rice Soup Mix (PAGE 27)	1/4 cup grated carrot
3 cups water	1 package Spice Mixture
1/4 cup (1/2 stick) butter	5 cups water
1 medium onion, chopped	1/4 cup sherry
1/2 cup chopped celery	

In a small saucepan, simmer the wild rice in the water for 35 minutes, or until tender. Drain, and set aside. In a soup kettle, melt the butter and cook the onion, celery, and carrot over low heat, until soft. Add the Spice Mixture, and stir well. Gradually add the water and stir with a whisk until the mixture thickens and is smooth. Add the wild rice and heat through. Just before serving, stir in the sherry.

Lone Star Chili Basket

This Lone Star Chili Basket makes a four-star house gift, especially for a winter visit. Featured is a Black Bean Chili Mix packed with six white porcelain chili bowls, a ladle, tortilla chips, a six-pack of Lone Star beer (tied with a bandanna), and six boot-shaped beer mugs — all cradled in a rattan log basket (PAGES *111-112*).

Black Bean Chili Mix

Makes 2 3/4 cups

2 cups dried black beans

Pack the black beans in an airtight container.

Spice Mixture

2 tablespoons dried oregano	1 1/2 tablespoons chili powder
1/4 cup all-purpose flour	1/2 cup ground cumin
4 chicken bouillon cubes, crumbled	1/2 teaspoon salt
2 tablespoons ground coriander seeds	1/2 teaspoon sugar

Combine the ingredients in a medium bowl and blend until they are evenly distributed. Store in an airtight container.

Black Bean Chili

Serves 10

1 package Black Bean Chili Mix (PAGE 29)
8 cups water
1/2 cup (1 stick) butter or margarine
1 cup chopped mild fresh chiles
1/2 cup chopped onion
1/2 cup chopped red bell pepper
1/2 cup chopped leek

3 cloves garlic, minced
1 package Spice Mixture
4 cups water
2 cups fresh corn, or equivalent of frozen, defrosted
4 cups shredded cooked turkey or chicken

In a large bowl, let the beans soak in water to cover them overnight. Drain the beans, combine them in a large pot with 8 cups of water. Bring the water to a boil, and simmer the beans uncovered for 2 hours. Drain and reserve the beans.

In a 6-quart stockpot, melt the butter over medium low heat, add the vegetables, and cook for 10 minutes, until they are softened. Add the Spice Mixture and whisk until the mixture is combined and bubbles. Stir constantly for 5 minutes, or until the flour (in the Spice Mixture) turns golden, then stir in the 4 cups of water. Purée one cup of corn and add to the chili. Add the remaining corn, chicken or turkey, and black beans. Simmer for 15 minutes, stirring occasionally, and season with salt and pepper. Serve immediately, or the chili will keep in the refrigerator for 3 days or frozen for 2 months.

Great Grains Basket

A delightful addition to anyone's pantry, this collection of rice and grain mixes can be the starting point for many creative menu ideas. Pack the mixtures into reusable, clear canisters and arrange them in a wooden basket lined with kitchen towels.

Brown Rice Pilaf Mix

Makes 2 cups

A deliciously different, nutty rice blend, this pilaf is excellent when served with chicken or fish.

2 cups brown rice

3 chicken bouillon cubes, crumbled

1 teaspoon salt

1/2 teaspoon freshly ground black pepper

1/2 teaspoon ground ginger

Combine and blend the ingredients in a small bowl. Store in an airtight container.

Brown Rice Pilaf

Serves 6

3 cups water

1 package Brown Rice Pilaf Mix

2 tablespoons currants

1/4 teaspoon cumin

2 tablespoons soy sauce

In a 2-quart saucepan, bring the water to a boil, and add the Brown Rice Pilaf Mix. Cover and reduce the heat and simmer for 25 to 35 minutes, until the liquid has been absorbed by the rice. Stir in the currants, cumin, and soy sauce. Serve immediately.

Pecan Rice Mix

Makes 2 3/4 cups

Using Basmati rice as a base for this blend gives it a flavor and aroma that is deliciously appealing. Serve Pecan Rice Mix with grilled game hens or duck.

4 chicken bouillon cubes, crumbled
1 tablespoon mustard seed
1 1/2 teaspoons grated lemon peel

1/2 teaspoon coriander
2 cups Basmati rice
3/4 cup pecan halves

Combine and blend the ingredients in a small bowl. Store in an airtight container.

Pecan Rice

Serves 8

4 3/4 cups water
1 package Pecan Rice Mix

In a 3-quart saucepan, bring the water to a boil and add the Pecan Rice Mix. Cover and reduce the heat to simmer. Cook for 20 minutes, or until the rice is tender and the liquid is absorbed.

Risotto with Sun-dried Tomatoes Mix

Makes 1 1/2 cups

This rice mix looks appetizing and colorfully decorative layered in an attractive glass jar.

1 cup Arborio rice

1/4 cup sun-dried tomatoes
(not packed in oil)

5 chicken bouillon cubes,
crumbled

Layer the ingredients in an airtight glass jar.

Risotto with Sun-dried Tomatoes

Serves 6

4 tablespoons butter, divided

1/2 cup chopped onion

1 package Risotto with Sun-dried
Tomatoes Mix

5 cups boiling water

1/4 cup grated Parmesan cheese

In a heavy-bottomed 4-quart saucepan, heat 2 tablespoons butter, then sauté the onion until it is translucent. Add the Risotto with Sun-dried Tomatoes Mix and stir to coat with the butter. Add 2 cups of boiling water; boil the mixture and continue to add water as it is absorbed. When all the water has been absorbed, stir in the remaining butter and Parmesan cheese. Serve immediately.

Couscous Salad Mix

Makes 2 cups

1 cup quick-cooking couscous   1 cup dried currants
1 chicken bouillon cube, crumbled   1/2 teaspoon dried cumin

Combine the ingredients in a small bowl and stir to blend. Store in an airtight container.

Couscous Vegetable Salad

Serves 4 to 6

Couscous Salad Mix   1/2 cup zucchini, diced
2/3 cup boiling water   1/4 cup olive oil
2 green onions, chopped   2 tablespoons lemon juice
1/2 cup red pepper, chopped

Place the Couscous Salad Mix in a bowl, and pour the boiling water over. Stir with a fork and let sit for 5 minutes, or until the water is absorbed. Stir in the green onions, red pepper, zucchini, olive oil, and lemon juice. Serve chilled or at room temperature.

Tabbouleh Mix

Makes 1 1/4 cups

1 cup bulgur (cracked wheat) 2 tablespoons dried mint
2 tablespoons dried parsley 1 chicken bouillon cube, crumbled

Combine the ingredients in a small bowl and stir to blend. Store in an airtight container.

Tabbouleh

Serves 6 to 8

Tabbouleh Mix 1 cup chopped tomatoes
2 cups boiling water 1/2 cup fresh lemon juice
1/2 cup minced onion 1/3 cup olive oil
1/2 cup minced parsley 1/2 teaspoon salt
1/2 cup minced fresh mint 1/4 teaspoon fresh black pepper

Place the Tabbouleh Mix in a bowl, and pour the boiling water over the mix. Let the mixture sit for 15 minutes. Drain through a sieve, and place the Tabbouleh Mix in a bowl. Add the remaining ingredients, and allow the tabbouleh to stand for about 30 minutes, or refrigerate if not using immediately. Serve at room temperature.

Backyard Barbecue Basket

Perfect for Father's Day or for inaugurating a new grill, this includes the two mixes that follow — beef and seafood rubs — plus skewers, assorted wood chips for smoking, a chef's apron, hat, matching oven mitts, and long-handled tongs and fork.

Cajun Beef Rub Mix

Makes 1/3 cup

2 tablespoons freshly ground black pepper
2 tablespoons garlic powder
2 tablespoons salt
2 tablespoons white pepper

1 tablespoon fennel seeds
1 tablespoon dry mustard
1 teaspoon paprika
1 teaspoon cayenne pepper

Combine the ingredients in a small bowl and blend until they are evenly distributed. Store in an airtight container.

Cajun Barbecued Beef

Serves 6

1/4 cup olive oil
1 tablespoon Cajun Beef Rub Mix

6 rib-eye steaks (about 3/4 inch thick)

Preheat the barbecue grill until coals have a white ash. Combine the oil and Cajun Beef Rub Mix in a large glass dish. Add the steaks and turn to coat. Allow the steaks to marinate in the oil mixture for one hour in the refrigerator. Grill the steaks to desired doneness.

Seafood Rub Mix

Makes 1/4 cup

An unusual blend of spices, this combination enhances the flavor of grilled fish.

1/2 teaspoon salt
1 teaspoon garlic powder
2 teaspoons paprika
1 teaspoon ground coriander

1/2 teaspoon ground cumin
1/4 teaspoon freshly ground black pepper
1/4 teaspoon dried lemon peel

Combine the ingredients in a small bowl and blend until they are evenly distributed. Store in an airtight container.

Grilled Fish Fillets

Serves 4

Use Seafood Rub on thick-fleshed fish such as swordfish, sea bass, or salmon.

4 fish fillets, cut 1 inch thick
(about 1/2 pound each)
1/4 cup olive oil

2 tablespoons lime juice
1 teaspoon Seafood Rub Mix

Place the fish fillets in a flat dish. Combine the olive oil, lime juice, and Seafood Rub Mix in a small mixing bowl, and paint the mixture onto the fish fillets. Cover with plastic wrap and refrigerate for 2 hours. Light the charcoal or preheat a gas grill. Remove the fish from the dish and grill over hot coals for 3 to 4 minutes per side, or until done. Remove from the grill and serve with additional fresh lime juice.

Bountiful Vegetable Basket

What better way to share the bounty of your garden than to give friends a large basket of fresh vegetables along with recipes for preparing them? Line the basket with a checkered cloth and arrange the assorted vegetables in artistic clusters, grouped around a little vase to hold fresh herbs.

Fresh Garden Medley

Serves 6

4 medium zucchini, cut into matchstick pieces

4 ears fresh corn, shucked, and removed from the cob

1 carrot, grated

3 tablespoons butter, melted

2 tablespoons fresh dillweed, or 1 tablespoon dried

Steam the zucchini and corn together for about 3 minutes, until the zucchini is crisp, but still tender. Transfer the mixture to a serving dish, and toss with the carrot, butter, and dillweed. Serve immediately.

Same-Day Pickles

Makes 12 cups

10 cups sliced cucumbers, zucchini, or summer squash (1/4-inch-thick slices)

1 large sweet onion, sliced (red for color is nice)

1 large sweet pepper, sliced in rings (red or yellow for color)

2 teaspoons salt

1 1/2 cups white vinegar

2 cups sugar

1 teaspoon pickling spice

1 teaspoon celery seed

Place the sliced vegetables in a large colander. Sprinkle salt over the vegetables and allow them to stand for 2 hours. Drain the vegetables well, and place in a large bowl. Heat the vinegar, sugar, and spices in a nonreactive saucepan until the sugar dissolves. Pour the vinegar mixture over the vegetables and refrigerate, covered, for at least 6 hours. Drain and serve. These pickles will keep in the refrigerator for up to 2 months.

Tea for Two Basket

A n antique teapot, tea strainer, matching teacups and saucers, and homemade tea mixes make a gracious gift when given in an old-fashioned wire basket, wrapped in antiqued tissue paper and tied with Victorian lace.

Citrus-Spiced Tea Mix

Makes 3/4 cup

Delicious hot or cold, Citrus-Spiced Tea Mix will stay and look fresh given in a pretty little metal canister.

1/2 cup tea leaves	6 whole allspice berries
12 whole cloves	3 1 1/2-inch cinnamon sticks, crushed
1 teaspoon dried lemon peel	

Combine the ingredients in a small bowl and blend until they are evenly distributed. Store in an airtight container.

Citrus-Spiced Tea

Serves 3 to 4

4 cups water
1 tablespoon Citrus-Spiced Tea Mix

Bring the water to a boil in a small saucepan or kettle. Place the Citrus-Spiced Tea Mix in a teapot, and pour in the boiling water. Let the mixture steep for 5 to 10 minutes. Serve hot, garnished with lemon slices.

Cranberry Apple Tea Mix

Makes 1 1/2 cups

1 cup dried cranberries   1/2 cup loose tea leaves (chamomile)
1/4 cup dried apples, chopped

Combine the cranberries, apples, and tea leaves in a small bowl. Store in an airtight container.

Cranberry Apple Tea

Serves 2 to 3

1/4 cup Cranberry Apple Tea Mix
4 cups boiling water

Place the Cranberry Apple Tea Mix into a teapot. Pour in the boiling water and let the mixture steep for 5 to 7 minutes. Serve hot.

Vive la France! Basket

That chic treat is a three-course French feast delivered in a wicker hamper lined with red tablecloth and navy blue napkins. For entrée, a Boeuf Bourguignon Mix (with recipe); for salad course, Gallic Salad Seasoning Mix; for classic Parisian dessert of bread, fruit, and cheese, a French Bread Mix and assorted cheeses plus fresh seasonal fruit. Round out the basket with two bottles of red wine (one for the stew, one to drink with dinner), and beribbon the hamper lid in red, white, and blue streamers tied around a wire whisk.

Boeuf Bourguignon Mix

1/4 cup

Nothing more than French beef stew with a fancy name, this dish is simple to make, yet special enough to be served to guests.

5 beef bouillon cubes, crumbled	1 teaspoon salt
1 bay leaf	1/4 teaspoon freshly ground black pepper
2 teaspoons dried thyme	

Combine the ingredients in a small bowl and blend until they are evenly distributed. Store in an airtight container.

Boeuf Bourguignon

Serves 8

3 pounds boneless beef stew meat, cut into 2-inch cubes

2 tablespoons canola oil

2 large onions, sliced

4 carrots, sliced into 1/2-inch rounds

3 large cloves garlic, crushed

1 cup chopped tomatoes

1 package Boeuf Bourguignon Mix

3 1/2 cups water

1 1/2 cups dry red wine

Preheat the oven to 325° F. In a 4-quart ovenproof casserole, over high heat, brown the meat in oil. Add the onions, carrots, garlic, and tomatoes. Reduce the heat to medium, stir the mixture, and cover, stirring occasionally, until the vegetables are crisp, but still tender. Add the Boeuf Bourguignon Mix, water, and wine. Bring the stew to a boil. Cover and bake for 2 to 3 hours, or until the meat is fork-tender. Remove the meat and vegetables from the pan, and remove as much fat as possible from the cooking liquid. Return the meat and vegetables to the pan. Taste the sauce and correct the seasonings. Serve the stew with steamed red potatoes and a green salad.

Gallic Salad Seasoning Mix

Makes 1/3 cup

1/4 cup dried tarragon

1 tablespoon dried thyme leaves

2 teaspoons dried basil

2 teaspoons dried dillweed

1 teaspoon salt

1/4 teaspoon freshly ground black pepper

Combine the ingredients in a small bowl and blend until they are evenly distributed. Store in an airtight container.

House Vinaigrette

Makes approximately 1 1/4 cups

1 cup olive oil   2 tablespoons Dijon mustard
1/4 cup white wine vinegar   2 teaspoons Gallic Salad Seasoning Mix

In a small bowl, whisk together the oil, vinegar, mustard, and Gallic Salad Seasoning Mix. Refrigerate before serving with mixed greens.

French Bread Mix

Makes 3 1/2 cups

A humble loaf of bread that becomes majestic when served with Boeuf Bourguignon or with assorted cheeses and wine.

3 cups all-purpose flour   1 teaspoon sugar
1/2 cup whole wheat flour   1 teaspoon salt
1 package dry active yeast

Combine and blend the ingredients in a medium bowl. Store in an airtight container.

French
Bread

Makes 2 loaves

1 cup lukewarm water (105°— 115°)
French Bread Mix

Preheat the oven to 400° F. Pour the water into a large mixing bowl. Add the French Bread Mix and stir until blended. Turn the bread out onto a floured board, and knead for 5 minutes, until it is smooth and elastic. Place the dough in a greased bowl, and cover with a sheet of plastic wrap. Let rise for 1 hour, until the dough is doubled in bulk. Punch the dough down and let it rise another hour, until it is doubled in size. Form the dough into 2 long loaves about 14 inches long, and place on a greased cookie sheet. Let it rise again for about 40 minutes. Bake the bread for 20 minutes. Check the loaves, and continue baking for another 10 minutes, or until they are golden brown and crisp. Remove the loaves to a rack and allow to cool. Serve warm.

Pasta Perfetto Basket

A large, bright-red enamelware colander holds four basics for everyone's favorite Italian meal: a package of imported pastas, a jar of homemade Sun-dried Tomato Pesto, a package of breadsticks, and a bottle of Chianti. An elaborate variation would include a pasta machine (Atlas hand crank), a bag of pasta mix for it, and some ingredients for duplicating your pesto: sun-dried tomatoes, extra-virgin olive oil, and a basil plant, all wrapped up in a checkered tablecloth.

Sun-dried Tomato Pesto

Makes 3 2/3 cups

1 cup sun-dried tomatoes, packed in oil, drained	4 tablespoons balsamic vinegar
6 garlic cloves	1/2 cup tightly packed fresh basil leaves
1/2 cup olive oil	1/2 cup flat-leaf parsley
	1 cup freshly grated Parmesan cheese

Combine all the ingredients in the work bowl of a food processor. Process for 15 seconds. Scrape the bowl, and process for 20 seconds. Remove the pesto from the bowl, store in a glass jar, and refrigerate until ready to serve. For each pound of pasta, use 1/4 to 1/3 cup pesto, tossed with hot noodles. Garnish with additional Parmesan cheese.

Basil Pesto

Makes 4 cups

2 cups tightly packed basil leaves	1/4 cup pine nuts
1 cup freshly grated Parmesan cheese	1/2 cup olive oil
3 garlic cloves	1/4 cup vegetable oil

In the blender of a food processor, process the basil, cheese, garlic, and pine nuts. With the machine running, gradually add the oils and process until smooth. Pour into a glass jar, and pour 1/2 inch olive oil on the top to seal the pesto. When ready to use, stir pesto and toss 1/4 to 1/3 cup pesto with 1 pound freshly cooked pasta.

Mardi Gras Basket

You don't have to be in New Orleans to celebrate Mardi Gras. This gift assembles its festive flavors in a stockpot for recipients to use in creating their own winter carnival table. The Peppered Pecans have just the right amount of spice to start off a delicious Cajun meal. The Gumbo Mix is a one-pot dinner that can be prepared in the pot. The Creole Seasoning Mix perks up any seafood dish. The feast can be finished off with vanilla ice cream smothered in Chocolate Praline Sauce. Decorate the pot with masks and Mardi Gras coins. Sprinkle purple, green, and gold confetti over the stockpot contents and wrap in brightly colored layered tissue with paper noisemakers tied on top.

Peppered Pecans

Makes 2 cups

1/2 cup sugar
1 tablespoon coarse salt
1 1/2 tablespoons freshly ground pepper
1/4 teaspoon cayenne pepper
2 cups pecan halves

Mix the sugar, salt, pepper, and cayenne in a small bowl. Heat a skillet over high heat. Shake the pecans in the skillet for one minute. Add half the blended mixture, shaking the skillet. When the sugar begins to caramelize, add the remaining mixture and shake the skillet constantly. Turn the pecans out onto paper towels to cool. Separate and store in an airtight container.

Gumbo Mix

Makes 2/3 cup

Whenever my husband and I tour New Orleans, we eat our way through the city. Gumbo happens to be one of our favorite foods, and this is one of the many ways we have enjoyed it.

1/2 cup all-purpose flour	1/2 teaspoon dried thyme leaves
1 1/2 teaspoons salt	1/2 teaspoon dried oregano leaves
1/4 teaspoon cayenne pepper	1 bay leaf, crushed
1/8 teaspoon freshly ground black pepper	5 chicken bouillon cubes, crumbled

Combine and blend the ingredients in a small bowl. Store in an airtight container.

Seafood Gumbo

Serves 8

1/2 cup vegetable oil	5 cups water
1 package Gumbo Mix	2 pounds mixed shellfish (shrimp, crab,
1 cup chopped onions	oysters, clams, or crayfish), cleaned
1 cup chopped green pepper	Chopped green onions
1 cup chopped celery	

In a large stockpot, heat the oil over medium high heat, and add the Gumbo Mix. Stir the mixture with a wire whisk, cooking about 3 minutes, until it is a dark amber color. Add the vegetables and stir for another 2 minutes. Cook over medium heat for 2 minutes more, and add the water. Whisk the gumbo, then stir constantly for about 7 minutes. If you plan to serve it later, remove from the stove at this time, and refrigerate. When ready to serve, bring the mixture to a boil and add the seafood. Reduce the heat and simmer for about 10 minutes. Remove from the heat, and skim off any accumulated oil from the top. Serve over rice, garnished with chopped green onions.

Creole Seasoning Mix

Makes 3/4 cup

This versatile seasoning spices up any dish, but is especially good with fish and shellfish.

1 cup salt
1/4 cup granulated garlic
1/4 cup freshly ground black pepper
1 teaspoon cayenne pepper

1/4 cup paprika
1 teaspoon oregano leaves
1 teaspoon thyme leaves

Combine and blend the ingredients in a small bowl. Store in an airtight container.

Cajun Shrimp Barbecue

Serves 4

24 large shrimp, shelled and deveined
12 tablespoons (1 1/2 sticks) butter, cold, cut into 1-inch pieces
1 1/2 teaspoons Creole Seasoning Mix

1/4 cup Worcestershire sauce
2 cloves garlic, chopped
1/4 cup lemon juice

Preheat the oven to 450° F. Place the shrimp in an ovenproof sauté pan. Dot with 6 tablespoons butter, Creole Seasoning Mix, Worcestershire, and garlic. Bake the shrimp for 3 to 4 minutes. Turn the shrimp, and bake for 2 to 3 minutes more. Transfer the sauté pan to the stove. Over medium-high heat, add the lemon juice and whisk in the remaining butter. Serve immediately with hot French bread for dipping.

Chocolate Praline Sauce

Makes 1 3/4 cups

This rich sauce is just the thing to serve over French vanilla ice cream. If you really want to be decadent, serve it over brownies topped with ice cream.

1/2 cup sugar
3/4 cup heavy cream
3 ounces bittersweet chocolate
chopped finely

1 teaspoon vanilla extract
1/2 cup pecan halves

In a heavy saucepan, cook the sugar over moderate heat until it begins to melt. Cook, stirring with a fork until it is fully melted, then cook, while swirling the pan, until it is golden caramel. Remove the pan from the heat, add the cream, then simmer until the caramel is dissolved. Add the chocolate and cook over low heat, whisking until the chocolate is melted and the sauce is smooth. Whisk in the vanilla, and stir in the pecans. Serve the sauce warm or at room temperature.

Cinco de Mayo Basket

T o celebrate this Mexican holiday, line a large basket with a serape or colorful tablecloth and tie dried red chile peppers on the handles of the basket. Include a lidded acrylic pitcher for the Margaritas Fantásticas, margarita glasses, coarse salt, gold tequila, limes, and a stoneware bowl for guacamole. You can take homemade guacamole along or bring the makings with you and prepare the guacamole at the party. Add a mariachi music tape, and you have the beginnings of a great party.

Guacamole

Makes 2 cups

4 Haas avocados
1 tomato, seeded and chopped
2 shallots, chopped
1 teaspoon lime juice

1 clove garlic, crushed
2 tablespoons chopped chiles
1 teaspoon salt

Peel and seed the avocados, then mash with a fork. Add the remaining ingredients, and stir to blend. Squeeze additional fresh lime juice over the surface of the guacamole to prevent discoloration. Serve with tortilla chips and fresh vegetables.

Margaritas Fantásticas

Serves 8

1 1/4 cups lime juice
1 1/2 cups José Cuervo Gold Tequila
1 1/4 cups Triple Sec

2 cups ice cubes
2 limes, quartered
Coarse salt

In the bowl of a blender, combine the lime juice, tequila, Triple Sec, and ice cubes. Blend until the mixture is slushy. Pour into prepared glasses — rims rubbed with a cut lime, then dipped in coarse salt, and chilled. Garnish filled glasses with a lime slice.

Wok on the Wild Side Basket

Fill a wok with the ingredients needed to make the Stir-fried Chicken and Noodles dish, along with a rice paddle, stir-fry spatula, and cleaver, plus a basic Chinese cookbook and six rice bowls, and six sets of chopsticks and chopstick rests. Include Chinese noodles (or vermicelli), vegetable oil, sesame oil, sesame seeds, soy sauce, rice wine vinegar, and cornstarch, which can be found in most supermarkets.

Stir-fried Chicken and Noodles

Serves 6

1/2 pound chicken cutlets, cut into 1/2-inch strips	1 cup chopped napa cabbage
2 teaspoons rice wine vinegar	1/2 cup chopped green onions
2 tablespoons soy sauce	1/2 cup sliced carrots
1 teaspoon cornstarch	1 (8-ounce) package Chinese noodles, cooked al dente
1/4 cup vegetable oil	3 tablespoons soy sauce
1 teaspoon chopped ginger	1 tablespoon sesame oil
1 clove garlic, chopped	1 tablespoon sesame seeds

Combine the chicken, rice vinegar, soy sauce, and cornstarch in a bowl. Refrigerate for 30 minutes. Heat 2 tablespoons vegetable oil on high heat. Add the chicken mixture and fry for one minute, or until the meat becomes light brown. Remove the chicken to a plate, and keep warm. Heat 2 more tablespoons vegetable oil and add the ginger and garlic. Stir-fry the garlic and ginger, stirring constantly. Add the vegetables and continue to stir-fry until crisp, but tender. Add the noodles and soy sauce and return the chicken to the wok. Stir-fry for 3 minutes. Add the sesame oil and sesame seeds and mix well. Serve immediately.

Let Them Eat Cake Basket

Marie Antoinette had the right idea when she uttered that famous line, and your friends will love you for giving them this selection of blue ribbon cake mixes. Use a Bundt pan, large flour sifter, or covered cake plate as your gift basket, and fill it with packages of your prepared cake mixes with recipe tags tied to each.

Carrot Cake Mix

Makes 5 2/3 cups

2 cups sugar	2 teaspoons baking soda
2 teaspoons powdered vanilla	1 tablespoon cinnamon
1/2 cup chopped pecans	1/4 teaspoon nutmeg
3 cups all-purpose flour	

Combine and blend the ingredients in a small bowl. Store in an airtight container.

Carrot Cake

Makes 1 13- by 9-inch cake

1 package Carrot Cake Mix	3 cups grated carrots
1 1/2 cups vegetable oil	1 (8-ounce can) crushed pineapple
3 large eggs	

Preheat the oven to 350° F. and grease a 13- by 9-inch baking dish. Place the Carrot Cake Mix in a large mixing bowl. Make a well in the center of the mix and add the oil, eggs, carrots, and pineapple. Blend until smooth. Pour into the prepared baking dish and bake for 40 to 50 minutes, or until a cake tester inserted into the center comes out clean. Cool the cake and frost if desired, or dust with powdered sugar.

Spiced Apple Cake Mix

Makes 6 cups

3 cups all-purpose flour

1 1/2 cups sugar

1 1/2 teaspoons baking soda

1 teaspoon powdered vanilla

1 1/2 teaspoons cinnamon

1/4 teaspoon ground nutmeg

1 cup chopped walnuts

1/2 cup golden raisins

Combine and blend the ingredients in a medium bowl. Store in an airtight container.

Spiced Apple Cake

Serves 8 to 10

1 package Spiced Apple Cake Mix

1 1/2 cups canola oil

3 large eggs

3 cups chopped apples

Preheat the oven to 350° F. and grease a tube or Bundt pan. Place the Spiced Apple Cake Mix into a large mixing bowl. Make a well in the center of the mix and add the oil, eggs, and apples. Stir until the mixture is smooth. Pour into the prepared pan and bake for 1 hour and 10 minutes, or until a toothpick inserted into the center comes out clean. Cool and remove from the cake pan.

Chocolate Brownie Cake Mix

Makes 7 1/2 cups

2 1/2 cups all-purpose flour
2 1/2 cups sugar
2/3 cup Dutch-process cocoa powder
(such as Dröste)

2 tablespoons instant coffee
2 teaspoons baking soda
1 1/2 cups walnuts
2 teaspoons powdered vanilla

Combine and blend the ingredients in a medium bowl. Store in an airtight container.

Chocolate Brownie Cake

Serves 8 to 10

1 package Chocolate Brownie Cake Mix
3 cups sour cream

2 large eggs
1/2 cup canola oil

Preheat the oven to 350° F. and grease a standard-size Bundt pan. In the large bowl of an electric mixer, place the Chocolate Brownie Cake Mix and add the remaining ingredients. Beat at medium low speed until the ingredients are smooth. Pour the batter into the prepared pan and bake the cake for 1 hour and 10 minutes, or until a cake tester inserted into the center comes out clean. Allow the cake to cool in the pan for 15 to 20 minutes, then remove it from the pan and cool on a wire rack. When the cake is completely cooled, refrigerate for easier slicing.

Chocolate Lover's Basket

I f you know a chocoholic like me who craves the stuff so much that there are days when nothing but chocolate will satisfy, pack up this chocolate-heaven gift. In two matching large mugs, place a package each of your White Hot Chocolate Mix and Mexican Hot Chocolate Mix, with recipe tags ribboned to the handles. Place them at each end of an oblong basket filled with your freshly baked Triple Chocolate Cookies and topped with a bar of imported semisweet chocolate and a gift subscription to *Chocolatier* magazine.

White Hot Chocolate Mix

Makes 1/2 cup

1/2 cup grated white chocolate or white chocolate chips

1 teaspoon dried orange peel

1 teaspoon vanilla powder

Combine and blend the ingredients in a small bowl. Store in an airtight container.

White Hot Chocolate

Serves 2

1 1/2 cups milk
1/4 cup White Hot Chocolate Mix

In a small saucepan, heat the milk until bubbles form around the outside. Add the White Hot Chocolate Mix and whisk until the chocolate is melted. Continue to whisk until the mixture is hot. Serve in heated mugs, or stir into strong hot coffee.

Mexican Hot Chocolate Mix

Makes 3 1/4 cups

1/3 cup light brown sugar   1/4 cup cocoa
3/4 teaspoon ground cinnamon   2 1/2 cups powdered milk
1 1/2 teaspoons powdered vanilla

Combine and blend the ingredients in a small bowl. Store in an airtight container.

Mexican Hot Chocolate

Serves 6

3 cups water   Cinnamon sticks for garnish
Mexican Hot Chocolate Mix

Heat the water to boiling and add the Mexican Hot Chocolate Mix. Stir with a whisk until the mixture is smooth. Divide the hot chocolate among mugs and garnish with cinnamon sticks. For a frothier hot chocolate, mix in a blender.

Triple
Chocolate
Cookies

Makes about 2 dozen

They are a soft, very rich chocolate cookie, flavored with cocoa, plus dark and white chocolate chunks. Reserve these for "chococonnoisseurs" only.

3/4 cup (1 1/2 sticks) unsalted butter softened to room temperature	1 1/2 cups all-purpose flour
2/3 cup sugar	1/3 cup cocoa
1/3 cup brown sugar	3/4 cup dark chocolate, chopped into 1/2-inch pieces
1 large egg	1/2 cup white chocolate, chopped into 1/2-inch pieces
1 teaspoon vanilla extract	

Preheat the oven to 325° F. Line two baking sheets with foil or waxed paper. In the large bowl of an electric mixer, cream together the butter and sugars until smooth. Add the egg and vanilla and continue beating. Add the flour, cocoa, and chocolate and beat at low speed until just blended. Roll the dough into golf-ball size and place 2 inches apart on prepared cookie sheets. Bake for 12 to 15 minutes, until the tops look dry. Cool on a wire rack for 3 minutes and remove to rack to cool completely.

Sundae Best Basket

Appropriate for any age group, you create an instant party atmosphere when giving this gift basket. On a large serving tray with handles, place a Donvier ice cream maker, a scoop, a set of old-fashioned sundae dishes, long-handled spoons, jars of homemade sauces, and assorted prepackaged toppings, such as nuts, candies, and a jar of maraschino cherries. Tie streamers and helium-filled balloons to the handles.

World's Best Hot Fudge Sauce

Makes 2 cups

Smooth, rich, glossy, and not too sweet, this is by far the world's best hot fudge sauce.

1/2 cup (1 stick) unsalted butter	1 1/2 cups sugar
4 ounces unsweetened chocolate	1 cup evaporated milk

In a small saucepan, melt the butter with the chocolate. Stir in the sugar, and add the evaporated milk, whisking until smooth. Remove from the heat. Store in an airtight container in the refrigerator. Reheat to serve.

Raspberry Sauce

Makes 5 cups

This sophisticated sauce is deceptively easy to make and delicious to taste. Try it over French vanilla ice cream.

4 cups fresh or frozen raspberries	2 teaspoons lemon juice
1 cup sugar	

Combine the ingredients in a small saucepan, and bring to a boil. Simmer for 3 minutes, stirring constantly. Taste the sauce and correct for sweetness. Strain through a fine sieve, and refrigerate in an airtight container until ready to use.

Milk Chocolate
Peanut Butter Sauce

Makes 1 3/4 cups

1 tablespoon butter

2 tablespoons light brown sugar

1 tablespoon light corn syrup

1/4 cup chunky peanut butter

1/2 cup heavy cream

3/4 cup chopped milk chocolate

In a small, heavy saucepan, melt the butter with the brown sugar and corn syrup over moderate heat. Whisk in the peanut butter and cream and bring to a boil. Add the chocolate and whisk the sauce until it is smooth. Serve warm over ice cream. Store in an airtight container in the refrigerator. Reheat to serve.

Pralines and Cream
Sauce

Makes 4 1/4 cups

Straight from New Orleans, this smooth sauce, studded with pecans, is perfect over ice cream.

1 1/2 cups sugar

3/4 cup light brown sugar

1/2 cup milk

6 tablespoons (3/4 stick) unsalted butter

1 1/2 cups pecan halves

1 teaspoon vanilla extract

Combine all the ingredients in a small saucepan and bring to a boil, stirring for one minute. Remove from the heat and pour into jars. Keep refrigerated. in an airtight container Reheat to serve.

Hooray
For the Red, White, and
Blue Basket

How lucky that just when we celebrate the Fourth of July, two of our flag's colors are in full bloom in fields where red and blue berries grow in abundance. Take advantage of that coincidence and build your gift to a holiday host around the berry pick of the season. Place little berry baskets filled with fresh raspberries, strawberries, blueberries, and boysenberries in a large flat basket lined with red-and-white checkered dish towels. The homemade mixes that follow are for recipes that include fresh berries. Pack these mixes in the basket in individual bags tied with tricolor ribbons to hold recipe tags.

Cobbler

Mix

Makes 2 cups

1 cup all-purpose flour   1 cup sugar
1 teaspoon baking powder   1 teaspoon powdered vanilla

Combine and blend the ingredients in a small bowl. Store in an airtight container.

Berry
Cobbler

Serves 8 to 10

4 cups fresh berries (blueberries raspberries, or boysenberries)

1/4 cup orange juice

1/4 cup sugar

1 teaspoon cinnamon

1 cup (2 sticks) unsalted butter, melted

1 egg

1 package Cobbler Mix (PAGE *60*)

Preheat the oven to 375° F. In a large mixing bowl, combine the berries, juice, sugar, and cinnamon. Place the berries in a 13- by 9-inch baking dish. In a small mixing bowl, blend the butter with the egg. Add the Cobbler Mix and stir until the mixture sticks together. Drop the cobbler topping by tablespoonfuls on top of the berry filling. Bake for 35 to 45 minutes, or until the topping is golden brown and the filling is bubbling. Allow to cool for about 15 minutes before serving.

Blueberry Popover
Pancake Mix

Makes 1 1/3 cups

I love popovers, pancakes, and blueberries, so when I came up with this mix, I was in heaven. The mix makes a pancake that tastes like a popover, but is baked in a 9-inch pie plate. It sends out luscious aromas when baking. What a wake-up call on a summer Saturday morning.

(continued)

1 teaspoon powdered vanilla	1/4 cup sugar
1/4 teaspoon salt	1 cup all-purpose flour
1/4 teaspoon ground nutmeg	

Combine and blend the ingredients in a small mixing bowl. Store in an airtight container.

Blueberry Popover Pancake

Serves 6

1 cup blueberries, boysenberries, or blackberries	1 package Blueberry Popover Pancake Mix (PAGE *61*)
1 cup milk	1/4 cup sugar mixed with 1 teaspoon ground cinnamon
2 tablespoons melted butter	
2 eggs	

Preheat the oven to 450° F. Butter a 9-inch pie plate and place the berries into the pan. Combine the milk, butter, and eggs in a blender or food processor fitted with the steel blade. Pulse on and off several times to blend the mixture. Add the Blueberry Popover Pancake Mix and process until the mixture is smooth. Pour over the berries and sprinkle with two teaspoons of cinnamon sugar. Bake 20 minutes. Reduce the oven temperature to 350° F. and bake until the pancake is golden brown, about another 15 or 20 minutes. Cut into wedges and serve immediately.

Strawberry Shortcake Mix

Makes 2 1/2 cups

My family's favorite Fourth of July dessert is strawberry shortcake. But these biscuits are delicious with any type of berry and can be spread with lemon curd and whipped cream when berries are not available.

2 cups all-purpose flour   1/2 teaspoon baking soda
2 teaspoons double-acting baking powder   1/2 cup buttermilk powder

Combine and blend the ingredients in a small bowl. Store in an airtight container.

Strawberry Shortcakes

Makes 8 shortcakes

1/2 cup vegetable shortening   1/4 cup sugar
1 package Strawberry Shortcake Mix   3 pints fresh strawberries, hulled and
2/3 cup water   quartered
1 cup heavy cream

In a small mixing bowl, cut the shortening into the Strawberry Shortcake Mix. Gradually add the water, stirring until the mixture forms a ball. Pat the dough into a round about 1/2 inch thick on a floured board. Cut 3-inch rounds out of the dough and place on a lightly greased baking sheet. Reroll any scraps and cut out rounds. You should have a total of 8. Bake the shortcakes for 10 to 15 minutes, until they are pale golden. Transfer to a wire rack. Cool to room temperature. In a small bowl, beat the heavy cream and the sugar until it holds a soft shape. Split the shortcakes in half horizontally, and spoon berries over the bottom half. Top with the some of the whipped cream, and arrange the tops of the shortcakes over the whipped cream. Serve immediately.

Thanksgiving Basket

Present these Thanksgiving essentials: homemade Dried Cranberry Sauce Mix, Pumpkin Pie Spice Mix, and a pot of fresh herbs for use in turkey stuffing in a pumpkin-shaped tureen. Another charming and budget-minded container is an oblong basket with rounded ends — the kind used for mushrooms. Line it with assorted whole nuts in their shells; put the little herb pot in the center, flanked by your packages of homemade mixes dressed in layered orange, yellow, and brown tissue with matching curly ribbon ties to which recipes are attached.

Dried Cranberry Sauce Mix

Makes 3/4 cup

1/4 cup brown sugar
1 tablespoon cornstarch
1 chicken bouillon cube, crushed

1/2 cup dried cranberries
1/4 teaspoon dried tarragon

Combine and blend the ingredients in a small bowl. Store in an airtight container.

Cranberry Sauce

Makes 1 3/4 cups

1/2 cup white wine
1 cup water
1 teaspoon balsamic vinegar

1 package Dried Cranberry Sauce Mix
1 tablespoon fresh parsley

In a small nonreactive saucepan, heat the wine, water, and vinegar over moderate heat. Whisk in the Dried Cranberry Sauce Mix and simmer, stirring occasionally, for 15 to 20 minutes. Stir in the parsley. Serve with pork or poultry. Refrigerate any leftover sauce.

Pumpkin Pie
Spice Mix

Makes 1/2 cup

A sprinkle of this into pumpkin or applesauce desserts adds just the right amount of spice.

1/4 cup ground cinnamon   1 tablespoon ground cloves
2 tablespoons ground ginger   1 tablespoon ground nutmeg

Combine and blend the ingredients in a small bowl. Store in an airtight container.

Pumpkin
Pie

Makes one 9-inch pie

2 eggs   1 1/2 teaspoons Pumpkin Pie Spice Mix
2 cups cooked pumpkin (or 1 16-ounce   1 2/3 cups light cream
can pumpkin puree)   1 9-inch pie shell
3/4 cup sugar

Preheat the oven to 425° F. In a large mixing bowl, whisk the eggs, pumpkin, sugar, Pumpkin Pie Spice Mix, and light cream together until the mixture is smooth. Pour the custard into the pie shell and bake for 15 minutes. Reduce the temperature to 350° F. and bake for another 45 minutes, or until a knife inserted into the center of the pie filling comes out clean.

Apple Sauce Cake

Makes 1 loaf

A stellar addition to anyone's recipe file, this cake improves with age.

1/2 cup (1 stick) unsalted butter, softened
1 cup sugar
1/2 cup brown sugar
1 cup applesauce

1/2 cup low-fat yogurt
2 cups cake flour
1 1/2 teaspoons Pumpkin Pie Spice Mix (PAGE 65)
2 teaspoons baking soda

Preheat the oven to 350° F. and butter a loaf pan. In a large bowl of an electric mixer, cream together the butter and sugars. Add the applesauce and yogurt, and blend until smooth. Add the cake flour, Pumpkin Pie Spice Mix, and baking soda. Stir to blend. Pour the batter into the prepared pan, and bake for 50 to 60 minutes, or until a toothpick inserted into the cake comes out clean. Cool the cake on a wire rack for 1 hour, and remove from the pan. Serve chilled.

Halloween Spooks Basket

What fun to bring this basket to a friend's home on that spookiest of nights. Goblins young and old will enjoy this fun assortment: small pumpkins for carving, fresh apples and caramels to make caramel apples, your homemade Peter's Pumpkin Bars and Caramel Nut Popcorn Balls. Include a copy of the book or audiotape *Scary Stories*, and pack it all in an over-the-arm-handled basket or big black canvas tote decorated with assorted Halloween stickers that will be handy for trick-or-treating.

Peter's Pumpkin Bars

Makes 40 bars

4 large eggs	2 cups all-purpose flour
1 2/3 cups sugar	2 teaspoons baking powder
1 cup oil	2 teaspoons Pumpkin Pie
2 cups cooked pumpkin (or 1 16-ounce	Spice Mix (PAGE 65)
can pumpkin puree)	1 teaspoon baking soda

Preheat the oven to 350° F. and grease a 15- by 10-inch jelly-roll pan. In the large bowl of an electric mixer, beat together the eggs, sugar, and oil. Gradually add the pumpkin, beating until smooth. Add the flour, baking powder, Pumpkin Pie Spice Mix, and baking soda, and stir until the mixture is smooth. Pour the batter into the prepared pan and bake for 25 to 30 minutes. Frost with Orange Frosting.

Orange Frosting

Makes 3 cups

1 3-ounce package cream cheese, softened	2 teaspoons orange extract
1/2 cup (1 stick) butter or margarine, softened	2 cups confectioners' sugar

In the small bowl of an electric mixer, beat the cream cheese and butter until smooth. Add the orange extract and confectioners' sugar, and continue to beat until the mixture is of spreading consistency. Frost cooled pumpkin bars.

Caramel Nut
Popcorn Balls

Makes 2 dozen 2-inch balls

2 quarts popped corn	1 cup light corn syrup
1 6 1/2-ounce can nuts (your choice)	1/2 cup (1 stick) butter or margarine
4 cups brown sugar	1/2 cup water

Combine the corn and nuts in a large pot. In a large heavy-bottomed pan combine the remaining ingredients. Bring to a boil and cook over medium high heat until the mixture reaches 290° F. on a candy thermometer. Pour the mixture over the combined popcorn and nuts, and stir until they are thoroughly coated. Roll the popcorn into balls and when cool, wrap individually in plastic wrap, and tie each with orange and black ribbons.

Caramel
Apples

Makes 4 to 5 apples

4 to 5 medium apples	48 caramel candies
Wooden sticks	2 tablespoons water

Wash and dry the apples. Insert a stick into the stem end of each apple. Melt the caramels with the water in a heavy saucepan over low heat, stirring frequently until smooth. Dip the apples into the hot caramel sauce, twirling until coated. Scrape excess sauce from the bottom of the apples. Place on waxed paper or foil sprayed with nonstick vegetable spray. Serve immediately or store in the refrigerator for up to two days. Let stand at room temperature for 15 minutes before serving.

Luck of the Irish Basket

Your favorite Irishman, Irishwoman, or just about anyone else will enjoy this gift on Saint Patrick's Day. Line a white plastic laundry basket with Kelly green tissue. Stuff a green napkin in each of four Irish-coffee glasses — the napkin corners prettily pointed out over the rim of the glass. Hang recipe tags for Irish Coffee and Nutty Irishman Coffee on handles of the glass holders and include ingredients for their blend: a bottle of Irish whiskey and a bag of fresh coffee beans. A coffee grinder and a shamrock plant complete this lucky gift assortment.

Irish Coffee

Makes 1 cup

1 tablespoon brown sugar   2 ounces Irish whiskey
6 ounces hot coffee   1/4 cup whipped cream

Place the brown sugar in a mug or Irish-coffee glass. Add the hot coffee and whiskey. Top with whipped cream and serve immediately.

Nutty Irishman Coffee

Makes 1 cup

1 ounce Frangelico liqueur   6 ounces hot coffee
1 ounce amaretto liqueur   1/4 cup whipped cream

Place the Frangelico and amaretto into a mug or heatproof glass. Add the hot coffee and top with whipped cream. Serve immediately.

Sweetheart Basket

Fresh strawberries, homemade Belgian Waffle Mix, a waffle iron (heart-shaped, ideally), a jug of pure maple syrup, each wrapped in red tissue and popped into a white canvas tote adorned with cutout red hearts, make a loving gift on February 14 — or whenever you want to say, "You're a sweetheart!" to someone who's done something wonderful for you.

Belgian Waffle Mix

Makes 2 1/4 cups

2 cups all-purpose flour
1 teaspoon salt

1 tablespoon baking powder
1 tablespoon powdered vanilla

Combine and blend the ingredients in a small bowl. Store in an airtight container.

Belgian Waffles

Makes 4 waffles

3 large eggs, separated
2 tablespoons butter, melted
1 cup milk
1 cup plus 2 tablespoons Belgian Waffle Mix

Maple syrup
Fresh strawberries
Whipped cream

In the small bowl of an electric mixer, beat the egg whites to soft peaks and set aside. In a large mixing bowl, combine the egg yolks, melted butter, and milk. Whisk in the Belgian Waffle Mix. Fold in the egg whites with a wire whisk. Bake in preheated waffle iron. Serve with warmed maple syrup or fresh strawberries and whipped cream.

Gingerbread House Christmas Basket

As symbolic of the holidays as tinsel on the tree and stockings on the mantel, a Gingerbread House Christmas Basket makes a cheerful gift for a whole family to share. A square basket is an ideal container, topped with a pointed roof made of cardboard to suggest the "house" inside. Add a cast-iron gingerbread plaque (Williams-Sonoma and other gourmet catalogs and shops have them), a package of homemade Gingerbread House Mix with directions for making it, a sack of powdered sugar for frosting, and assorted candies for decorating the completed house.

Gingerbread House Mix

Enough dough to make one house

2/3 cup light brown sugar	1/2 teaspoon ground cinnamon
6 cups all-purpose flour	1/2 teaspoon ground ginger
2 teaspoons baking soda	1/2 teaspoon ground nutmeg
1/2 teaspoon ground cloves	1 teaspoon salt

Combine all the ingredients in a medium bowl and use a whisk to blend. Store in an airtight container.

Gingerbread House

1 package Gingerbread House Mix (PAGE 71)

1 cup molasses

1/4 cup milk

1/2 cup (1 stick) butter or margarine, softened

Place the Gingerbread House Mix in a large bowl. Make a well in the center of the mix and add the butter, molasses, and milk. Stir the batter until the mixture begins to leave the sides of the bowl. Turn it out onto a floured board and knead. It should be stiff. Press the dough onto one side of a well-greased gingerbread house plaque. Bake at 350° F. for 20 minutes or until browned. Remove the pieces from the mold and cool on a rack. Allow the plaque to cool before doing the other side. Repeat with the other side of the mold. Allow the gingerbread to cool completely before assembling the house.

Frosting

Makes 4 1/4 cups

2 egg whites

4 cups confectioners' sugar

In a small bowl of an electric mixer, beat the egg whites and confectioners' sugar until stiff. Cover the frosting until ready to use.

Assembling the Gingerbread House

Our family constructs gingerbread houses every Christmas and we have found that assembling the walls the night before helps to stabilize the house. A cardboard cake board makes a good base for it. Adorn the roof before attaching it to the decorated house. This is a wonderful time to put a child's imagination to work. The frosting allows much freedom for error, and even with the youngest children, cracks can be camouflaged with "snow." For a squeeze-tube effect, put the frosting into zip-type sandwich bags, cut the corner, and the bag acts as your decorating tube. Embellishments can be traditional candies, shredded wheat cereal for a thatched cottage look, or use cereals such as Chex for roofing materials.

Happy Hanukkah Basket

Hanukkah is one of the most joyful festivals in the Jewish calendar. It is a family event where music, games, and delicious food combine for an eight-day celebration. Traditional foods include potato pancakes, assorted vegetables, and roasted beef brisket. Your homemade Beef Brisket Marinade Mix is an appropriate contribution to the feast. Place it in a white basket lined with royal blue napkins and include a bottle of wine, candles for the menorah, and for the kids, a dreidel (spinning top) and chocolate coins covered in gold foil.

Beef Brisket Marinade Mix

Makes 1/4 cup

8 juniper berries, crushed	1 teaspoon dried thyme
2 bay leaves	1 teaspoon salt
1 1/2 teaspoons dried basil	1/4 teaspoon pepper
1 teaspoon dried rosemary	1 teaspoon garlic, dried

Combine and blend the ingredients in a small bowl. Store in an airtight container.

Beef
Brisket

Serves 8

1 750-ml bottle dry white wine	1 5-pound flat cut beef brisket
1 cup port wine	2 tablespoons vegetable oil
1/2 cup chopped onions	1 onion, chopped
4 large garlic cloves, chopped	4 carrots, sliced
1 package Beef Brisket Marinade	2 ribs celery, chopped
Mix (PAGE 74)	4 cloves garlic, chopped

Combine the wines, onions, garlic, and Beef Brisket Marinade Mix in a medium saucepan, and bring to a boil. Place the brisket in a 13- by 9-inch glass baking dish. Pour the marinade over the brisket. Cover and refrigerate overnight.

Preheat the oven to 300° F. Drain the brisket from the marinade. Heat the oil in an ovenproof pan, and add the brisket. Cook the meat, browning evenly on all sides. Add the vegetables and continue to sauté for about 4 minutes, until the vegetables are soft. Cover the pan and bake in the oven for about 4 hours. Remove the brisket from the pan, and remove the fat from the pan juices. Slice the meat thinly across the grain. Strain the pan juices and correct for seasoning. Pour the pan juices over the brisket. Serve with potato pancakes.

Auld Lang Syne

R ing in the New Year with a festive and imaginative beverage assortment for a holiday host. In a zippered food tote — the insulated silver-fabric double-handled one is perfect — place three bottles: Grandpa Jim's Eggnog Mix prepared and bottled by you, recipe attached; flanked by two bottles of dry red wine, with a Glühwein Mix package and recipe tied to one and a Glögg Mix package and recipe tied to the other. Add a nutmeg grater and bag of whole nutmeg and tie paper party hats and noisemakers to the tote handles.

Grandpa Jim's Eggnog Mix

Makes 1 quart

1 1/2 cups bourbon 2 whole nutmegs
1 1/4 cups dark rum 4 large cinnamon sticks
1 1/4 cups brandy 8 whole cloves
2 vanilla beans, halved lengthwise

Pour the liquor into an attractive one-quart bottle. Add the spices and cork the bottle. Allow to stand in a cool, dark place for 2 weeks. This mixture will keep for 4 months.

Eggnog

Serves 8

8 egg yolks   1 cup Grandpa Jim's Eggnog
1/2 cup sugar   Mix (PAGE 76)
2 1/2 cups whipping cream, chilled

In the small bowl of an electric mixer, beat together the egg yolks and sugar until the mixture is pale yellow. Add the whipping cream and continue to beat. Add Grandpa Jim's Eggnog Mix and blend. Serve immediately, garnished with grated nutmeg and additional whipped cream.

Glühwein
Mix

Makes 2 1/4 cups

A Bavarian drink traditionally served as an after-ski warmer, this will be a welcome treat during the holidays.

2 cups sugar   1 teaspoon cloves
1 1/2 teaspoons cinnamon   1/2 teaspoon nutmeg
1 tablespoon whole allspice

Combine the ingredients in a small bowl and blend until the spices are evenly distributed throughout the sugar. Store in an airtight container.

Glühwein

S e r v e s   4   t o   6

1 750-ml bottle dry red wine
1/2 cup Glühwein Mix (PAGE 77)

In a small, nonreactive saucepan, heat the wine and blend together over medium heat, stirring to dissolve the sugar in the Glühwein Mix. Serve in tempered glass mugs.

Glögg Mix

M a k e s   1   1 / 2   c u p s

A Swedish drink that includes raisins and almonds, this pungent drink will warm up any winter night.

3/4 cup raisins
1 tablespoon whole cardamom
1 tablespoon whole cloves

2 sticks cinnamon, broken into pieces
1/2 cup sugar

Combine and blend the ingredients in a small bowl. Store in an airtight container.

Glögg

S e r v e s   4   t o   6

1 750-ml bottle dry red wine
1 1/2 cups water
1 package Glögg Mix

2 tablespoons raisins
1 tablespoon sliced almonds

Combine the red wine and water in a medium saucepan with the Glögg Mix. Bring the mixture to a boil and strain into mugs. Garnish with raisins and almonds.

❀ SPECIAL OCCASION

B A S K E T S

This section is for gift givers who enjoy observing events, big or little, in the lives of dear friends, family members, and business colleagues — beyond birthdays and anniversaries. Did your favorite uncle just buy a new car? Did your best friend adopt a cat? Is your football-fan neighbor off to a Super Bowl weekend? There's a gift basket in the following pages for each — and dozens more.

Conventional baskets aren't the only containers to use when designing a gift. Canvas tote bags, wooden boxes, laundry baskets, hampers, backpacks, magazine racks, log baskets, mini vegetable baskets (the little green plastic ones that hold cherry tomatoes — the oblong wooden ones that mushrooms come in) can all be adapted to your gift needs. Your teenager hasn't been near that tricycle in the garage for a dozen years? Rescue that basket hanging on the handle-bars, clean it up, and fill it up with garden tools for a summer hostess gift. Magazines for a hospital gift? Shoeshine equipment for a college grad entering the corporate world?

Decorating your package is a nice way to personalize it. Stickers, rubber stamp designs, and confetti can be used. Using stencil designs, you can paint baskets, totes, and other containers with motifs that convey the theme. An ordinary shoe box covered in foil paper and lined with shredded Mylar looks like it came from a chic boutique. A fabric-lined basket can last for years as a functional and decorative household accessory. To affix the fabric, fold over its raw edge and smooth with an iron. Use a glue gun on the wrong side of the fabric, then attach it to the inside of the basket rim. If the basket has an open rim and/or handles, weave ribbon through it.

Whatever creative direction your packages take, your perfect basket gifts are sure to bring pleasure to giver and receiver alike.

✿ *Bubble Bath*

Just what the doctor ordered for a stressed-out friend, this pamper package is also a great Mother's Day gift. Line a white basket with a bath towel of appropriate color and nestle the following items inside, each wrapped and ribboned in tissue paper that follows the color scheme. If you're really feeling flush — or if it's a group gift — include a terry-cloth robe on a satin-padded hanger.

Loofah
Back scrubber
Nail brush
Manicure set
Washcloths and hand towels
Bath beads
Bubble bath
Body lotion
Scented candle with holder
Cassette tape with soothing music, perhaps ocean sounds or soft jazz
Magazines

❁ Gardener's Helper

B
A
S
K
E
T

The classic English gardening basket isn't the only kind suited to this gift. Plastic shopping baskets or totes also make wonderful receptacles for this Gardener's Helper Basket. This gift is a fine way to launch children into the satisfying and educational hobby of watching the food they eat grow in their own backyard.

Gardening shears
Mister
Hand rake
Spade
Seeds for vegetables and herbs
A basic gardening book
Garden gloves
Kneeling pad
Gift certificate to a nursery

✿ *Kitchen Table Office*

B
A
S
K
E
T

For that "kitchen-table office" where your friend does the household accounts and other domestic paperwork, this thoughtful gift provides basic equipment. Assemble the smallest items in a recycled little square basket (the green plastic one that holds cherry tomatoes is a good size), lined with brightly colored tissue. Or, if your gift includes all the items on the following list, an office "In" box would do the job. The last few items on the list are for personal correspondence and fancy invitation-addressing work.

Package of pencils
Assorted pens (in colors), markers, highlighters
Plain paper
Envelopes
Roll of postage stamps
Post-It notes
Address book
Scotch tape
Mini stapler
Mini calculator
Rubber stamps for decoration and stamp pads (in color)
Small calligraphy pen set
Initial seal with wax
Embossing kit

Welcome Neighbors

B
A
S
K
E
T

Your new neighbors have just moved in. They're up to their necks in packing crates. They'd like to clean the kitchen before putting their dishes away, but where did they pack those cleaning supplies? The doorbell rings, and it's you to the rescue. Your good-neighbor gift? A big bucket filled with lots of old rags and all the basics for the immediate move-in cleanup chores. And when they sit down to take a break from that hard work, they'll find the useful items you've included, shown at the bottom of the following list, to help them get acquainted with their new neighborhood. Put a sash of wide satin ribbon around the bucket and finish if off with a great big bow.

Lots of old rags
Scouring pads
Sponges
Cleanser (powder and liquid)
Glass cleaner
Brushes (include a toothbrush — great for cleaning tiny crevices)
Rubber gloves
Roll of paper towels
Bar of soap
Map of the area marked with the locations of your favorite restaurants, dry cleaners, etc.
Subscription to local magazine or paper
A card listing store recommendations and local services (baby-sitters, snow removal, swimming-pool service)

Guest Bath

B
A
S
K
E
T

A welcome for overnight guests, this basket contains all the things they might forget to bring. Use a round, handled basket, line it with four washcloths, and fill it with these grooming essentials.

Sample sizes of shampoo and conditioner
Soap
Spray deodorant
Bath beads
Shower cap
Hand lotion
Talcum powder
Disposable razor
Shaving cream
Toothpaste
Toothbrush
Folded kimono, tied with ribbon
Slippers (disposable paper)
Current magazine, rolled and tied with ribbon

✿ Dirty Duds

B

Just the gift for someone moving into his or her first apartment. Fill a large, colorful laundry bag with these essentials. (Ironing board accompanies it.)

A

S

Laundry detergent

Liquid soap for delicate fabrics

All-fabric bleach

K

Fabric softener

Stain remover

2 dozen plastic hangers

Mesh bag for delicate clothes

E

Roll of quarters

Steam iron

T

Ironing board

❀ Kitchen Beginner

Help a novice cook get a handle on a start-up kitchen by providing the many little basic implements needed. Since these tools all — literally — have handles, make a bouquet of them ribboned together upright in the utensil basket of a sink dish drainer. The final larger items at the bottom of the list can be individually wrapped and arranged in the dish drainer. Include your favorite basic cookbook.

1 whisk
2 rubber spatulas
3 wooden spoons
Ladle
Slotted spoon
Long fork
Tongs
Paring knife
Slicing knife
Vegetable peeler
Can opener
Kitchen scissors
Corkscrew
Small plastic cutting board
1 small mixing bowl
1 medium mixing bowl
Cheese grater
Measuring cups and spoons

❀ New Car

B

For the friend who has a new car, or for the boss who has everything, fill a plastic tote with a selection from the following list and adorn the handles with ribbons.

A

S

Car wash gift certificate

Local service station gift certificate

Automobile club gift certificate

Chamois

Car wash sponge

Bottle of interior cleaner

Spray can of tire cleaner

Tire brush

Tire gauge

Jumper cables

Flares

Flashlight

Key chain

Spare-key compartment

Road maps

First-aid kit

Anti-theft lock

Driving gloves

K

E

T

# New Pet

B
A
S
K
E
T

To welcome a new member to the family, use an animal bed as your basket and fill it with Fido or Fifi's essentials. Wrap each in white tissue paper that has been stamped with black paw prints.

Small chewing toy
Scratching post (if a kitty)
Animal treats
A bag of pet food
Pet shampoo
Book about pet care
Leash and collar
Personalized animal tag
Copy of James Herriot's **All Creatures Great and Small**

 # Off to College

B
A
S
K
E
T

Since my daughter, Carrie, leaves for college soon, we came up with this practical send-off gift. As there's never enough storage space in a dorm room, we packed everything in a large plastic milk crate.

Portable cassette player with batteries
Prerecorded and blank cassette tapes
Hair scrunchies
Journal and pen
Rolls of quarters for laundry
Stationery, postcards, and stamps
Pocket-sized day planner
Wall calendar highlighted with special family dates and events
Stuffed animal

 *Newborn*

B
A
S
K
E
T

Welcome a newborn with this assortment of bathing essentials given, of course, in a useful portable baby tub. Line it with a hooded bath towel and tuck the items in, thin satin ribbons tied around each. The soft items look pretty rolled and ribboned.

Baby washcloth
Hooded bath towel
Baby sleeper
Baby soap
Baby lotion
Baby shampoo
Baby nail clippers
Package of newborn diapers
Brush and comb
Rattle
Rubber ducky

Baby, Too

This gift caters to an older baby's mealtime needs. Pack the items in a small stackable tote that can be kept on the bottom shelf of a high chair. After placing the individually wrapped items in the tote, wrap the whole thing up with a small plastic tablecloth that can be slipped under and around the high chair at mealtime to protect the floor and catch those inevitable food spills. The cloth is then easily emptied and wiped down after each meal.

B
A
S
K
E
T

2 bibs

2 baby spoons (one for baby to hold, one for feeding)

Baby bowl

Compartmented baby plate

Personalized bottle

Lidded cup

Small rubber squeeze toy with suction-cup base for high-chair tray

Parents'

B
A
S

All the equipment that must go along is provided in this useful gift that will accompany parent and child to the store, the park, or on a visit to Grandma's. Once called a diaper bag (when I was a new mom), today's greater variety of multipocketed totes can be outfitted to be serviceable right up through the toddler stage. Choose one with a long shoulder strap that will fit over the stroller.

K
E
T

Disposable diapers
Changing pad
Baby wipes
Ziploc bags for disposables
Travel bottle
Lidded plastic cup
Bib
Pacifier
Teething toy (on long ribbon to attach to stroller)
Rattle (on long ribbon)
Lightweight blanket
Sun hat
Baby sunglasses
Baby suntan lotion
Small box of tissues
Small board books

❀ On the Road Again

B
A
S
K
E
T

When I was a child, my parents took the family on many long driving trips. My aunt used to pack baskets with things for us to do in the car. The rule for our trips was that we could unwrap only one item at a time, and at given intervals we were able to open others. Keeping track on the car clock helped us to tell time and also allowed us time to enjoy each item in the basket.

In selecting items, consider the gender and age of the children, as well as the length of the trip. To hold the items, I chose a backpack and wrapped each item in colored tissue paper.

Drawing/writing pad
Washable crayons
Coloring book
Playing cards
Stamps with stamp pads
Books
Travel-size games
Small portable cassette player with extra batteries
Prerecorded cassette tapes
Disposable camera
Map to keep track of the trip
Travel diary and pencil

✿ Teen Summer Survival Kit

B
A
S
K
E
T

Fill a big beach bag with these ingredients for summer fun — a terrific birthday or high-school graduation gift.

Cassette audio tapes (recorded book or teen's favorite music)
Books (one classic, one current nonfiction)
Frisbee
Suntan lotion
Thongs
Sunglasses
Beach towel
Plain visor and puffy paints to decorate it with a dimensional effect
Gift certificates to the local yogurt shop
Discount tickets to local movie theater

❀ Sun and Sand

B
A

Living near the beach, our beach basket is always filled and ready to go. A natural as a housewarming basket for owners of a beach home, this gift also makes a sunny send-off for seaside honeymooners. For the couple, divide up the items into two packages and give his and hers matching shoulder totes.

S
K
E
T

2 beach towels
2 folding beach mats
Suntan lotion
Sunglasses
Visors
Masks and snorkels
Inflatable beach ball
Smash ball set
Frisbee
Compact radio/cassette player with dual headsets
Travel-size Scrabble
Individual water bottles

❀ Petit Picasso

B
A
S
K
E
T

A gift to tap into a child's creativity, this basket will keep youngsters busy for hours. Pack these items in a canvas tote that can be decorated with fabric paints.

Puffy paints (for dimensional effects)
Fabric paints
Fabric crayons
Colored pens and pencils
White cotton hat to paint
T-shirt to decorate
Doodle art poster
Stencils
Large pad of newsprint paper
Painting smock
Glue
Package of felt squares
Yarn
Package of beads

❀ Sunday Painter

B
A
S

As change-of-pace therapy for the workaholic or inspiration for a retirement hobby, this starter kit for watercolor painting is best delivered in a fishing tackle box with a hinged lid, handle, and interior compartments for separating brushes, tubes, etc. Tackle boxes come in a variety of colors. Art supply and hardware stores are good places to find such wooden, plastic, or metal boxes.

K
E
T

Basic assortment of tube watercolors
Paintbrushes in assorted sizes
Watercolor pencils
Erasers
Sketchbook
Block of watercolor paper
Pastel crayons
Apron or smock
Paint rags
How-to book on watercolor painting
Water bottles for cleaning brushes

Teddy Bear's Picnic

B
A
S
K
E
T

A charming idea for a child's birthday party, this basket with its cuddly teddy bear theme will delight even teenagers. Make sure to decorate the party area with teddy bears of all shapes and descriptions. Line a large picnic basket with bear-motif fabric or wrapping papers and include the following items.

Paper plates, cups, and napkins with a bear theme
Bear ears for each guest (available at party shops)
The book The Teddy Bear's Picnic *(with cassette)*
Box of teddy bear cookies for each guest
Bag of Gummi Bears for each guest
Small teddy bear for each guest

 # Camper's Backpack

Designed for the novice or experienced camper, this outfitted backpack is filled with just the right basics to take along on a trip to the great outdoors.

B
A
S
K
E
T

Flashlight
Water bottle
Swiss Army knife
Folded poncho
Cup and spoon
Trail mix
Compass
Gift certificate to a camping store
Guide to backpacking in the local area

Sports Fan

B

My son, Ryan, is a sports fanatic. He loves to play sports, but also loves to watch the pros. This is his idea of the perfect gift for a sports fan. Use a plastic can with a lid (in favorite-team colors if possible) or decorate the outside of the can with sports logos.

A

S

Small, soft-sided insulated cooler for drinks

K

Insulated mug with team logo

Favorite team sports cap

Team pennant

E

Large bag of peanuts

Nerf football

Whiffle ball-and-bat set

T

Tickets to an upcoming game

Sports encyclopedia

 *Super Bowl*

B
A
S
K
E
T

A close relative to the Sports Fan Basket, this gift is only for the diehard football fanatic. Outfit a backpack with these stadium standbys and decorate the straps with pom-poms in team colors.

Bag of pretzels
Bag of popcorn
Canned beer or sodas
Team hat
Team T-shirt
Plastic cups with team logos
Tear-apart referee doll (sold in novelty stores)
Season's program for favorite team

Guests' Bedside

B
A
S
K
E
T

A unique gift to leave in a hotel room, this basket will provide a welcome for clients visiting your city or for out-of-towners invited to the wedding or other big party you're giving. Free tourist brochures are available through your local chamber of commerce or visitors' bureau. If your city is famous for something special, try to gear your choice of basket or souvenirs in the basket in that direction. For example, in Philadelphia, adorn your basket with a little Liberty Bell.

Local maps (with attractions highlighted)
Tour ticket to see local attractions
Discount tickets to local attractions
Tokens or passes for public transportation
Local magazine with week's events listed
Printed card with important phone numbers and recommended restaurants
Schedule of events (for wedding or clients) and directions to each
Fresh fruit
Snacks (local specialties or small bags of pretzels, chips, candy bars)
Bottle of wine or sparkling cider

Vintage Wine / Cheese Connoisseur

B A S K E T

With many friends or coworkers chipping in to share the expense, this deluxe wedding gift can launch newlyweds on a pleasurable lifelong hobby as wine and cheese connoisseurs. Select a wooden or steel wine rack, and have your local wine shop help choose some vintages that will mature timed to celebrate first, fifth, tenth, and ongoing milestone anniversaries. Label the bottles for those occasions and fill the rest of the rack with other fine, mature wines. Line an accompanying round basket with mylar or excelsior and place the following items in it. Wrap the basket in clear cellophane tied with streamer ribbons to which a corkscrew is attached.

Subscription to a food magazine
Wine bottle stoppers
4 white wineglasses
4 red wineglasses
Wine coasters
Assorted crackers
Gift certificate to local cheese shop
Corkscrew

Al Fresco

B A S K E T

For tots through senior citizens, everyone enjoys an al fresco spread — whether it's on a picnic table at the lake, on the grass or sand at a park or beach, or on a tailgate at the stadium. Line a lidded hamper with a forty-inch-square tablecloth and four matching napkins. Coordinate lightweight acrylic tableware available in a range of festive colors.

4 acrylic wineglasses

4 acrylic plates

4 acrylic dessert bowls

4 lightweight place settings, plus 2 serving spoons

4 napkin rings

4 insulated acrylic mugs

Thermos for hot beverages

Plastic food containers

Acrylic salt and pepper mills

Bottle of wine

Corkscrew

Gift certificate to local gourmet market to fill the basket

 *Bye -Bye*

B
A
S
K
E
T

When I think of a typical basket, I picture those sent to ship staterooms with wine, fruit, and candy. Those, plus other delicacies, are in the list below — a fine bon voyage gift for honeymooners as well as other ship travelers. Line a large square basket with straw, nestle the items in place, sprinkle with confetti, then seal with beribboned cellophane. Or, though less traditional than a basket, a zippered tote makes a thoughtful package for the honeymoon suite or to be tucked into the backseat of the "getaway" car. The travelers then have a handy fold-up bag for use on their return trip to bring home all the purchases they have gathered along the way.

Bottle of champagne
Jar of caviar
Package of crackers
Assorted fresh fruit
Assorted candies
Pair of disposable champagne flutes
Tour book of destination

 *Guy /Gal Friday*

B
A

To show gratitude to a valued assistant on Secretary's Day or to mark his or her anniversary with the company, fill a colorful accordion file with some special desk accessories, plus some personal grooming items that are handy to have in the office, a sweet treat, and a gift certificate.

S
K
E
T

Personalized Post-It notes
Mont Blanc pen
Letter opener
Hand lotion
Small mirror
Small box of fine chocolates
Gift certificate for any (or a few) of these services: facial, manicure, haircut, tanning salon, massage

 # Relax a Boss

B
A
S
K
E
T

Every boss needs a little stress release and comedy relief during the business day. This whimsical gift should do it. Pack this assortment in a plastic wastebasket with a big happy-smile face chalked on the side.

Palm-fitting rubber fidget balls (à la Captain Queeg)
Basketball hoop for wastebasket
Swedish foot massager (wooden balls, sole of foot rubs on it)
Back scratcher
Desk games
Funny Post-It notes
Funny coffee mug filled with anti-stress vitamins

❀ Apple for the Teacher

B
A
S
K
E
T

This "you are appreciated" gift is sure to receive an A+ from teacher. Start with a shallow rectangular basket or file tray that becomes a useful desk accessory for collecting test papers. Playing on the apple theme, fill with the items that follow. Have your child participate by creating apple-decorated wrapping paper (with crayons or stickers) that goes around the package.

Red and green pencils
Post-It notes decorated with apples
Teacher's stamps with stamp pads
Bags of apple chips
Apple-flavored jelly beans
2 large red apples
Mug decorated with apples (buy plain mug and decorate it yourself with paint pens)
Cinnamon-apple tea bags

 # Get Well

B
A
S
K
E
T

For that friend at home in bed with the flu or to perk up a hospital patient's spirits, try to find a whimsical basket possibly in the shape of an animal and fill it with the helpful pastime gifts listed below.

Nonalcoholic sparkling cider
Assorted magazines
Books on audiocassette
Movie videotape
Stuffed teddy bear (comfy companion for any sickbed)
Doodle art poster and felt tip pens
Crossword puzzle book
Thank-you notes with stamps

Source Guide

COOK FLAVORING COMPANY
P.O. BOX 890
Tacoma, WA 98401
(206) 627-5499
Vanilla powder

SACO FOODS, INC.
P.O. BOX 5461
Madison, WI 53705
Buttermilk powder

SELECT ORIGINS HERBS AND SPICES
BOX N
Southampton, NY 11968
(800) 822-2092
*Excellent selection of herbs,
spices, dried cherries,
and cranberries.*

THE GREEN HOUSE
P.O. BOX 231069
Encinitas, CA 92023-1069
(619) 942-5371, ext. 114
Call for a location near you.

BASKETVILLE
Main Street
P.O. BOX 710
Putney, VT 05346
(800) 258-4553
*Handcrafted woven wooden baskets,
wooden buckets, pails,
maple sugar buckets,
and Shaker-style baskets.*

EUCALYPTUS STONEWARE
2201 San Dieguito Road
Del Mar, CA 92014
(619) 755-5656
*Manufacturers of oven-to-table
ceramic baskets.*

THE WOODEN SPOON
P.O. BOX 931
Clinton, CT 06413-0931
(800) 431-2207
*Donvier ice cream maker,
kitchen supplies, and porcelain.*

CRATE AND BARREL

P.O. BOX 9059

Wheeling, IL 60090-9059

(800) 323-5461

*Picnic hampers, garden trugs,
log baskets, magazine racks,
bamboo boxes, wine racks,
porcelain, and glassware.*

WILLIAMS-SONOMA

P.O. BOX 7456

San Francisco, CA 94120

(800) 541-1262

*Cookware, baskets,
cooking tools, glassware,
porcelain, linens,
and gourmet foods.*

HOLD EVERYTHING

P.O. BOX 7807

San Francisco, CA 94120-7807

(800) 421-2264

*Plastic cans, totes, shelf baskets,
pantry baskets, decorated tins,
and many other containers.*

GARDENER'S EDEN

P.O. BOX 7307

San Francisco, CA 94120-7307

(800) 822-8600

*Gardening supplies,
fancy garden accessories,
seeds, plants, and containers.*

JESSICA'S BISCUIT

P.O. BOX 301

Newtonville, MA 02160

(800) 225-4264

Cookbooks

GIFT BASKET

REGISTRY

Date	Name	Occasion	Gift

GIFT BASKET

Date	Name	Occasion	Gift

REGISTRY

Date	Name	Occasion	Gift

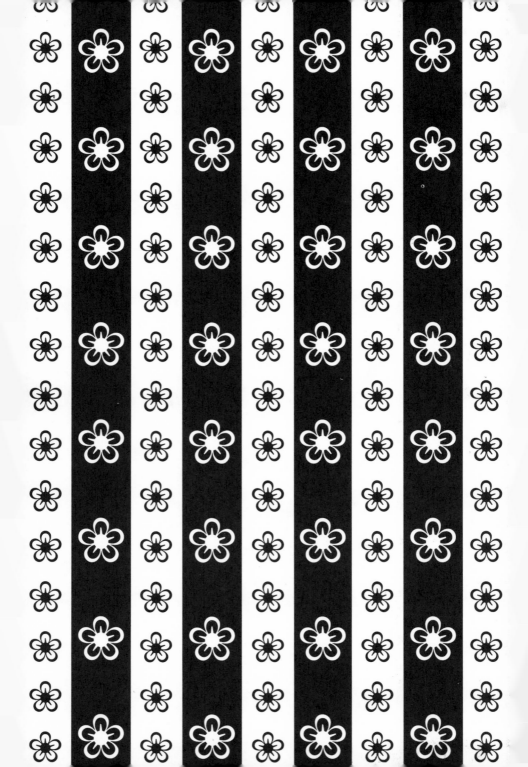